Beginning Game Development with Amazon Lumberyard

Create 3D Games Using Amazon Lumberyard and Lua

Jaken Chandler Herman

Apress®

Beginning Game Development with Amazon Lumberyard: Create 3D Games Using Amazon Lumberyard and Lua

Jaken Chandler Herman
Conroe, TX, USA

ISBN-13 (pbk): 978-1-4842-5072-3   ISBN-13 (electronic): 978-1-4842-5073-0
https://doi.org/10.1007/978-1-4842-5073-0

Managing Director, Apress Media LLC: Welmoed Spahr
Acquisitions Editor: Spandana Chatterjee
Development Editor: Matthew Moodie
Coordinating Editor: Shrikant Vishwakarma

Cover designed by eStudioCalamar

Cover image designed by Freepik (www.freepik.com)

Distributed to the book trade worldwide by Springer Science+Business Media New York, 233 Spring Street, 6th Floor, New York, NY 10013. Phone 1-800-SPRINGER, fax (201) 348-4505, e-mail orders-ny@springer-sbm.com, or visit www.springeronline.com. Apress Media, LLC is a California LLC and the sole member (owner) is Springer Science + Business Media Finance Inc (SSBM Finance Inc). SSBM Finance Inc is a **Delaware** corporation.

For information on translations, please e-mail rights@apress.com, or visit http://www.apress.com/rights-permissions.

Apress titles may be purchased in bulk for academic, corporate, or promotional use. eBook versions and licenses are also available for most titles. For more information, reference our Print and eBook Bulk Sales web page at http://www.apress.com/bulk-sales.

Any source code or other supplementary material referenced by the author in this book is available to readers on GitHub via the book's product page, located at www.apress.com/ 978-1-4842-5072-3. For more detailed information, please visit http://www.apress.com/ source-code.

Printed on acid-free paper

*To my amazing wife, family,
and friends for supporting me
along this journey.*

Table of Contents

About the Author

 **Jaken Chandler Herman** is a software engineer living in Texas. Jaken holds a bachelor of science in computer science with a focus on software engineering from Sam Houston State University. Outside of university, Jaken worked as a software engineering contractor at NASA. He has worked with many different and new technologies and has an ever-expanding wealth of information on all topics related to programming. In game development, he has academic experience as well as hands-on hobbyist experience having created many mobile-based games, a side-scrolling platformer, and a racing game.

About the Technical Reviewer

Dominique Regalado is a computer science graduate from Sam Houston State University with interests in full stack architecture, cloud platform technologies, and game development. She currently works as an associate software engineer, so providing insight for those new to software development is one of her passions. She has attended hackathons, career fairs, and even the renowned Grace Hopper convention to spread knowledge. Assisting in the authoring of this book was just another great opportunity to learn about a new engine while passing along the knowledge discovered.

CHAPTER 1

Install and Setup of Amazon Lumberyard

You are about to embark on an amazing journey. A journey in which you will be creating your very first video game in Amazon Lumberyard. This will be an extremely rewarding and likely humbling experience. Through my many failed attempts at creating video games when I first began working on them, I often found myself having so much information thrown at me that it was seemingly impossible to figure out where to start, what pieces of the information were *actually* important to my specific project, and where to look for advice and questions along the way.

Lucky for you, however, this book will walk you through everything, from the beginning all the way to the *game over* screen. Before we can begin, we need to go through the setup process.

Required Components Outside of the Lumberyard Engine

Amazon Lumberyard requires a few components outside of those that come packaged with it. One of the great things about Amazon Lumberyard is that the required components are completely free, so you do not need to worry about any additional costs in your game development endeavors. You can develop a video game on a AAA engine completely and 100% for free.

© Jaken Chandler Herman 2019
J. C. Herman, *Beginning Game Development with Amazon Lumberyard*,
https://doi.org/10.1007/978-1-4842-5073-0_1

Note   AAA, pronounced "Triple-A," is an informal classification used for video games typically to denote higher budgets and higher quality of development. Think of AAA as a way of saying "Blockbuster," as you would with movies. While in this book we likely won't build a AAA game, Amazon Lumberyard easily supports developing such games.

There are a few *optional* components, however, that do have a price tag attached to them, but for the purposes of this book, we will ensure that everything is free of charge along the way.

Installing Visual Studio

The first component we will install and set up is going to be Visual Studio, an IDE made by Microsoft.

Note   IDE stands for "Integrated Development Environment," which is just a software application that aids programmers (like you) in creating their own software. These integrated development environments typically consist of tools like a source-code editor (like a notepad), debugging system, and a build automation suite, to name a few.

Installing Visual Studio will allow us to select certain C++ development packages that Amazon Lumberyard will require for compiling the game code. Don't worry, we are not going to be writing any C++ in this project; the engine just requires C++ compilers and libraries to be installed.

On your web browser of choice, navigate to `https://visualstudio.microsoft.com`. Note that there will be many options for Visual Studio. Microsoft typically releases a new edition every other year, so at the time of your reading this, there may be a new edition out. For this book, we will be using Visual Studio 2017 although any future editions will still suffice when the 2017 edition becomes antiquated. Do not get too hung up on editions of external software; if Amazon Lumberyard supports it, just take the latest version.

Be careful not to download *Visual Studio Code*. While both are made by Microsoft, Visual Studio and Visual Studio Code are not the same application. Visual Studio Code is a more lightweight text editor that has some debugging features, and Visual Studio is a fully fledged IDE packed with features for developing, testing, and deploying projects built in many different frameworks and languages. Visual Studio Code will not come bundled with the necessary development components that Visual Studio provides.

Under the area labeled "Visual Studio IDE," click "Download for Windows," and you will be greeted with three options: Community, Professional, and Enterprise. Any of these will work, but for the purposes of this text, we will be selecting the Community edition (as it is the free option). Professional and Enterprise editions are more feature-rich and suitable for more advanced software development outside of the scope for development of a simple game. For new developers, the environment may be more overwhelming than necessary. Select "Community," and your download will begin.

Run the .exe executable that you just downloaded in order to install the Visual Studio Installer. If prompted by a window asking, "Do you want to allow this app to make changes to your device?", select "Yes." You will now be looking at the main GUI for the Visual Studio Installer.

Note   GUI stands for "Graphical User Interface," and it is exactly that – an interface with graphics that allows users to interact with software systems through means of visual indicators like graphical icons, buttons, and photos.

This is where we will select what we need, where to install what we need on our machine, and what we feel comfortable leaving behind. Select the tiles "Desktop development with C++," "Game Development with C++," and "Linux Development with C++," pictured in Figure 1-1, then select "Install" in the bottom-right corner of the window.

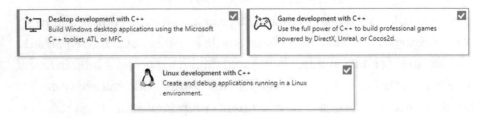

Figure 1-1. *These tiles represent the required C++ components needed to compile game code in Amazon Lumberyard*

You will now have a working copy of Visual Studio as well as the required C++ additional components installed on your machine.

Installing the Amazon Lumberyard Engine

Now that we have Visual Studio Community 2017 installed, it is time to install and set up the main software program we will be using throughout the book – Amazon Lumberyard. Navigate to https://aws.amazon.com/lumberyard/downloads. Click the button that says "Download Now" under the tile currently titled as "Lumberyard Beta 1.17," but just remember that version numbers do change, so the page title may be different at the time of your reading this. Download the latest version of Amazon Lumberyard and launch the executable when prompted, keeping in mind that it is required that you will be using a Windows machine running Windows operating system 7 or higher.

Currently, Amazon Lumberyard is not wholly supported on Macintosh systems, despite Lumberyard Mac Support Files available on the download page. This download will include some source code and tools required to build and run the Lumberyard game engine for developers creating macOS, iOS, and Android games on a Macintosh. However, the Asset Processor, Lumberyard Editor, and Remote Shader Compiler will require Windows 7 or later in order to build game assets and edit levels. If you want to run commands from your Macintosh's terminal, you must have access to a computer with a version of Amazon Lumberyard installed.

Note   Any hardships you may encounter along the way of your environment setup can likely be resolved by navigating to the Amazon Lumberyard documentation currently available at `https://docs.aws.amazon.com/lumberyard`. If a solution still cannot be found, try developer forums like `https://gamedev.amazon.com/forums` or even the popular Game Development Stack Exchange QA site, `https://gamedev.stackexchange.com`, searching via the "lumberyard-engine" question tag.

Once you have downloaded the LumberyardInstaller[versionnumber].exe file, navigate to it in your file system and double-click it in order to launch the executable. After the initial install process, click the button that says "Launch Lumberyard Setup Assistant." The Lumberyard Setup Assistant will greet you with two options: express install and custom install.

Express Install

Express install will give you everything you need to get started with the Amazon Lumberyard Editor, and it will allow you the option to come back to the Setup Assistant later to add in any plugins you may want, as well as SDKs that you may need to add to your project that were previously unconsidered.

Note   SDK stands for "Software Development Kit," which is a set of development tools that allows developers to create applications for certain software frameworks, platforms, or packages. For example, the development of an Android app on a Java platform requires developers to install the Java SDK.

Custom Install

Custom install allows you to select any plugins or SDKs at the time of your installing Amazon Lumberyard. For the purpose of the project, we will want to select this installation type. Click the orange *Customize* button in the *Custom Install* tile in the Lumberyard Setup Assistant, shown in Figure 1-2.

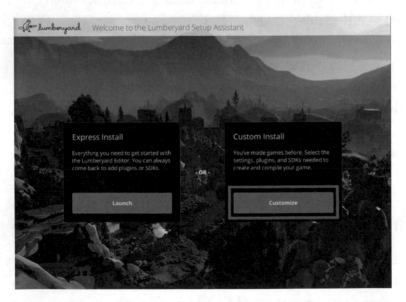

Figure 1-2.   *The first interaction with Amazon Lumberyard Setup Assistant we will have – selecting a custom install*

You will be presented with a few groups of checkboxes. Each item on the left submenu is a group, and each group will have a selection of checkboxes that relate to that group's categorical text.

Get Started

First the *Get Started* tab will pop up, and there will be a subtitle *What do you want to do with Lumberyard?* displayed. By default, the "Run your game project" and "Run the Lumberyard Editor and tools" options will be selected. If these options are not selected, go ahead and select them now, along with the "Compile the game code," "Compile the engine and asset pipeline," and "Compile the Lumberyard Editor and tools" options, as these will be the five options we will need. We are not going to select any other options for now. Under the subtitle *Visual Studio Version* in the "Get Started" group we are already on, we are going to choose the "Visual Studio 2017" option (deselect any other version if chosen by default). Again, keep in mind that because Visual Studio versions will change, you should select the option that corresponds to the Visual Studio platform you installed earlier in the chapter. Figure 1-3 shows which selections we will have made in the "Get Started" group, assuming "Run your game project" and "Run the Lumberyard Editor and tools" options were already selected. Click the orange *next* button in the bottom right corner to advance to the next group of the Amazon Lumberyard Setup Assistant, titled *Install Software*.

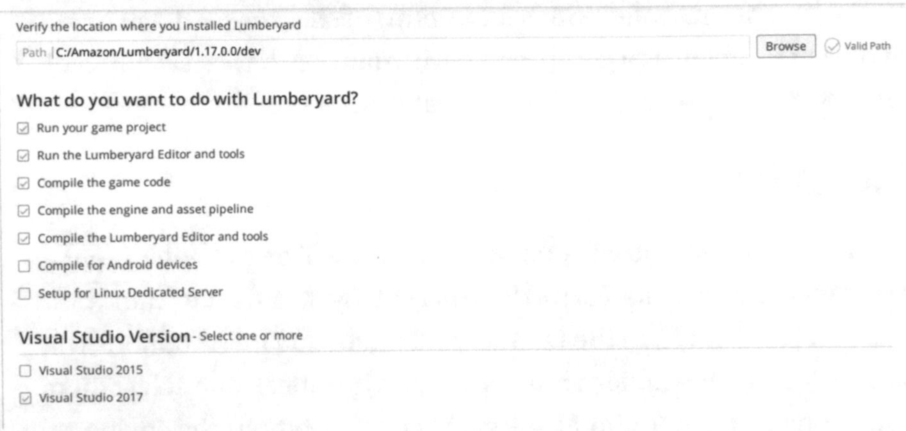

Verify the location where you installed Lumberyard

Path | C:/Amazon/Lumberyard/1.17.0.0/dev   Browse   ⊘ Valid Path

What do you want to do with Lumberyard?

☑ Run your game project

☑ Run the Lumberyard Editor and tools

☑ Compile the game code

☑ Compile the engine and asset pipeline

☑ Compile the Lumberyard Editor and tools

☐ Compile for Android devices

☐ Setup for Linux Dedicated Server

Visual Studio Version - Select one or more

☐ Visual Studio 2015

☑ Visual Studio 2017

Figure 1-3. *The necessary selections to make in the "Get Started" group of the Amazon Lumberyard Setup Assistant*

Install Software

The required software for Amazon Lumberyard includes *Microsoft DirectX Redistributable*, which allows multimedia-rich applications to run on Windows-based machines, as well as *Visual C++ Redistributable for Visual Studio 20XX* and *Visual Studio 20XX*. Note here that I put "20XX" because you will need the Redistributable packages for whichever Visual Studio platform you chose to use. This package will install runtime components that are required to run C++ applications, which Amazon Lumberyard will be building in the background.

Ensure that all fields under the required software subtitle are installed, by checking the "Status" column of those fields. If the software is installed, you will see a green check mark in this column, and if the software is not installed, you will see a red X. If the software is partially installed, or perhaps the version of the software is out of date or deprecated, you will see a yellow warning sign. All three of these symbols are shown in Figure 1-4.

Figure 1-4. *The status column of required and optional software fields shows a green check mark if the software is installed, a red "X" if the software is not installed, or a yellow warning indicator if the software is partially installed or requiring an update*

Optional software includes *Audiokinetic Wwise LTX Authoring Tool*, which is an advanced, interactive sound engine for games, *FFmpeg*, which is video encoding software, and *SpeedTree for Lumberyard*, which is a program for modeling and real-time rendering of trees and plants. We will not be opting to install any of the optional software for our game; thus, we will just leave these programs uninstalled and ignore this section of the Amazon Lumberyard Setup Assistant.

Once your required software packages are all installed and showing the green check-mark indicator, click the orange *Next* button in the bottom right-hand corner of the screen to move on to the *Install Required SDKs* group of the Setup Assistant.

Install Required SDKs

Need a break? This is one of the easiest steps of the entire setup of Amazon Lumberyard. This is where we will install all of our required SDKs, including SQLite, RapidJSON, MD5, and, of course, Lua. The Amazon Lumberyard Setup Assistant has made this step a breeze by adding a "Install all" button at the top of this group. You will see a button titled "Browse" above the "Install all" button next to an entry field titled "Third-party path." Click the "Browse" button, and select the directory in which you would like to install all these SDKs. If you are okay installing them in the default location, do not worry about this step. Go ahead and click the "Install all" button now, shown in Figure 1-5, in order to install all the required SDKs for our game development process.

Required SDKs | Install all | ([6.74 GB] of disk space required for this download)

Figure 1-5. *The required SDKs are the easiest part to install when setting up Amazon Lumberyard, due to this "Install all" button*

Grab some popcorn, this may take a while. You can see the progress of your SDK downloads in the bottom left-hand side of the Lumberyard Setup Assistant window, shown in Figure 1-6. Like the "Install Software" group earlier, the Required SDKs table has a column labeled "Status" that will show the green check mark if the SDK has been installed, a yellow warning indicator of the SDK has only been partially installed or requiring an update, or a red "X" if the SDK is not installed.

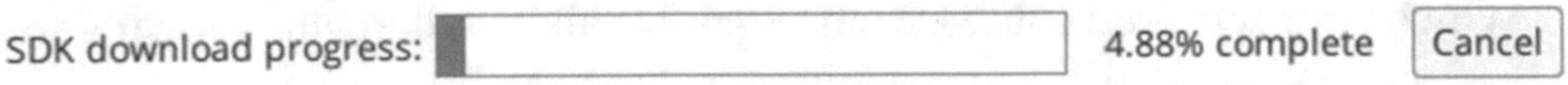

SDK download progress: [   ] 4.88% complete | Cancel |

Figure 1-6. *The SDK download progress bar shows the percentage of required SDKs that have successfully been downloaded*

Once all your required SDKs have been installed, click the orange Next button in the bottom right-hand corner of the screen to move on to the Install optional SDKs group of the Setup Assistant.

Install Optional SDKs

Like the "Install Required SDKs" group, there will be an entry field labeled "Third-party path" and a "Browse" button in order for you to select where you'd like any optional SDKs to be installed; however, unlike the "Install Required SDKs" group, there is no convenient "Install all" button. That is okay, as there is only one of the optional SDKs we will need. At the time of writing this, the Clang SDK is considered optional in the Lumberyard Setup Assistant, but it is required to create new projects and open them in the Lumberyard Editor. Select the orange "Install SDK" button next to the

Clang option, shown in Figure 1-7, if you do not already have a version of Clang on your computer. Again, you will see the blue progress bar in the bottom left-hand corner of your screen while the SDK installs. As stated earlier, we will not be using any other optional SDKs, although, after you have finished the book and have become an Amazon Lumberyard wizard, I would highly recommend you come back and install some of these SDKs to implement some more advanced functionality into your project.

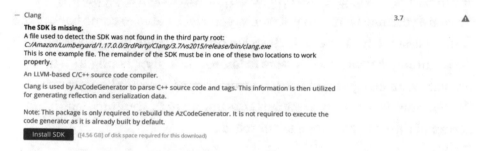

Figure 1-7. *While the Lumberyard Setup Assistant claims that Clang is an optional SDK, it is required to built your project and engine*

One of the more interesting optional SDKs is the Twitch Commerce SDK, which provides access to social functions, login, chat, and other APIs associated with the famous livestreaming service Twitch.

Because we will not be utilizing anymore of the available optional SDKs, select the orange Next button in the bottom right-hand corner of the screen to continue to the "Install Plugins" group.

Install Plugins

In the "Install Plugins" group, we have the option to install popular content creation software like various versions of Autodesk Maya, Adobe Photoshop, and Autodesk Max, as well as RC Shell Commands. We also have the option, instead of installing these programs, to locate them on our hard drive if we were to have them already installed on our machines.

We are not going to need any of these plugins for the purposes of this project, although I would again recommend that you come back to this page and experiment once you are more familiar with the engine.

Click the orange *Next* button in the bottom right-hand corner of the screen to continue to the final group of the Amazon Lumberyard Setup Assistant – "Summary."

Install Optional Software The final group of the Amazon Lumberyard Setup Assistant will give you one final option to install any optional software you may want. Do not worry, you will be able to come back to the Setup Assistant even after it is closed in order to install these again later in the future. You will now be able to launch the editor, configure a new project, or enable gems, which are extensions of Amazon Lumberyard.

For now, let's click the orange *Close* button in the bottom right-hand corner of the screen to finalize our setup.

Running the Lumberyard Editor

Next, we will run the Lumberyard Editor. Press the Windows key, type "Lumberyard Editor," and select the Lumberyard Editor Icon to launch the software. You may, depending on your user status on your personal machine, be greeted with a Windows Defender Firewall Security alert saying that some features of the application have been blocked. In order to allows all editor features to work as intended, select the "Allow Access" button if this happens.

Summary

Congratulations, you have just completed the setup of the Amazon Lumberyard engine. In the next chapter, we will learn to navigate the engine, focusing on helpful keyboard shortcuts, pane navigation, and other general terminology related to the program.

CHAPTER 2

Navigating the Engine

Now that you have Amazon Lumberyard installed on your computer, this chapter will walk you through the layout of the engine. We are going to talk about pane navigation, some useful hot keys to help you stay more efficient in your work, and some terminology of engine-related topics. We still will not be creating any game elements or logic yet, as it will be more beneficial for us to navigate through the environment and learn the ins and outs of the Amazon Lumberyard engine before we try to jump into development mode.

Open the Engine

The first, most obvious step we will need to take is opening up the engine. While it sounds easy enough, there are a few different ways to do it, and there are some conflicts that arise if you have multiple versions of Visual Studio on your computer. Because Amazon Lumberyard is in beta, it is possible that these conflicts will be resolved within the next year or two, but for now, let us walk through the process of opening the engine in a few different ways.

© Jaken Chandler Herman 2019
J. C. Herman, *Beginning Game Development with Amazon Lumberyard*,
https://doi.org/10.1007/978-1-4842-5073-0_2

Note Beta is the second phase of the software development life cycle. The beta phase generally begins when software is seemingly complete but likely contains a few unknown bugs. The benefit of beta testing is that it allows users to find bugs by using the software in a way the developers previously had not thought of.

The first method, and likely the easiest if your computer only has one version of Visual Studio, is through the start menu. Click the Windows icon or press the Windows key on your keyboard to open the start menu. Type "Lumberyard Editor" and select the gray Amazon Lumberyard logo, shown in Figure 2-1.

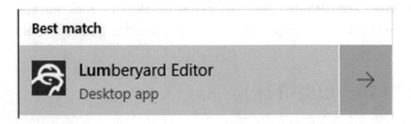

Figure 2-1. *While the Lumberyard Setup Assistant claims that Clang is an optional SDK, it is required to built your project and engine*

If all goes well, you may automatically be signed in to your Amazon account. If you are not automatically signed in, the startup of the Lumberyard engine may prompt an Amazon Login at this point. If you have made it to this stage, you have started up the engine, and you are ready to get to work. If this fits your case, move on to the next section, titled "INSERT_TITLE_HERE." If this did not work for you, keep reading, and we will come to a solution.

If you got an error message saying, "An error occurred while loading gems ... please build the current project before attempting to run Asset Processor again", shown in Figure 2-2, followed by an error about the

CrySystem not initializing properly and the CrySystem not being able to initialize, do not panic. This is a very solvable problem.

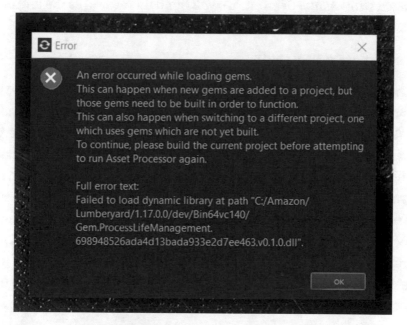

Figure 2-2. *A common error to receive when first running the Amazon Lumberyard Editor states "To continue, please build the current project before attempting to run Asset Processor again"*

Open up Powershell by clicking the Windows icon or by pressing the Windows key on your keyboard, type "Powershell," and select the blue Powershell icon.

Navigate to the Amazon Lumberyard dev directory by running the following commands:

```
cd C:\
cd Amazon\Lumberyard\1.17.0.0\dev
```

Then, run the `lmbr_waf` batch file to build the game and engine. Even though we have not created a game project, Amazon Lumberyard comes packaged with a game demo, so we will build this as well as the engine. To run the batch file, run the following command in your Powershell:

```
.\lmbr_waf game_and_engine
```

The process of building the game and engine may take a while, so grab a cup of coffee and prepare to watch a few online videos while you wait (or read ahead). Once the build is complete, attempt to open the Lumberyard Editor again through the start menu. If everything worked out, you have the engine running and you are ready to begin. If that's you, move on to the next section titled "INSERT_TITLE_HERE." If you are still getting the same error message from Figure 2-2, there is another remedy to the situation, so do not worry. If you do not still have your Powershell open, reopen it from the start menu (or via the keyboard combination Windows key + "X" at the same time, then "I") and run the following commands to navigate to the Amazon Lumberyard dev\Bin64vc141 directory:

```
cd C:\
cd Amazon\Lumberyard\1.17.0.0\dev\Bin64vc141
```

Next, run the `editor.exe` executable file to launch the editor:

```
.\editor.exe
```

The editor will begin to open and will succeed this time. The reason this works is because if you were getting the error in Figure 2-2 before, it was due to the Asset Processor's inability to load the dynamic library in the directory Amazon\Lumberyard\1.17.0.0\dev\Bin64vc140, which the Amazon Lumberyard Editor sometimes uses by default. Bin64vc140 DLLs are from Visual Studio 2015, and for this book, we have chosen to use Visual Studio 2017; therefore, we need Bin64vc141 DLLs. Feel free to continue to the next section titled "INSERT_TITLE_HERE," while I go through one more method of opening the Amazon Lumberyard Editor.

Note   A DLL, also known as a dynamic-link library, is like an executable file, but they are not *directly* executable. DLLs are Microsoft's implementation of a shared library. They contain functions, classes, variables, and other components that an .exe or another DLL uses. So, while users cannot run DLLs directly, other programs can use them as references.

Another way to open the editor outside of the main way, which I showed you earlier in the chapter, is through the Amazon Lumberyard Setup Assistant. If you look back at Chapter 1, in the "Summary" group, there is an option at the top of the screen with an orange button that says, "Launch Editor." Clicking this button will do exactly that.

Pane Navigation

Now that the Amazon Lumberyard Editor is open, it is time to dig in and play around a little bit. You will see a window that says, "Welcome to Lumberyard," which has options for creating new levels, opening existing levels, and changing your current project. Amazon comes installed with a starter game that allows seasoned game developers a chance to play around with the engine without having to come up with an idea for a new game, create new artwork, and sink tons of time and energy into the project. For now, we're going to ignore this, so click the "x" in the top right-hand corner of this window. Now you will have an empty editor with no entities, no game artwork or wireframes in the viewport window, nothing in the console, and nothing in the Asset Browser. If any of that terminology went over your head, don't worry, I am going to introduce you to all of it in this chapter.

Introduction to the Viewport

To start off, allow me to introduce to you the first, most useful window in the entire Lumberyard editor – the viewport. The viewport is where we will align, place, scale, and add all entities and objects to our game. It is also where the game will be played when the "Play Game" button is selected. The viewport is the large window in the middle of the editor. While it looks deceptively simple, navigating the viewport can be tricky at times to get an object in the proper alignment with your camera and therefore will take a bit of practice, so let us go over a few controls that will help you work more productively while making your game.

First, click and hold the right-click button on your mouse within the viewport, and while holding, drag your mouse around. As you will notice, this allows you to look around the viewport as if you were standing stationary in one spot of the viewport. This comes in handy when you need to look at entities from multiple different angles.

In order to zoom in and out on the viewport in order to get an up-close of an object, or perhaps to back out far enough to see your game from bird's-eye view, scroll down on your mouse scroll wheel or your trackpad for zooming in, and scroll up on your mouse scroll wheel or trackpad for zooming out. Think of this as either pulling the objects closer by scrolling down or pushing the objects in the viewport away by scrolling up.

To select an object within the viewport rather than the Entity Outliner, left-click the object within the viewport, and your object will be highlighted in both the viewport and the Entity Outliner. You can now use various tools in the toolbars we will discuss further in this chapter to modify this object. If you want to make changes to multiple objects at once, simply hold down your left-click button and drag along the viewport. This will select any objects that exists in the rectangle your mouse has just created, with your starting point being the angle opposite of your endpoint.

There will be a point in time that your game gets so many objects it may be hard to find the one you want, and even when you do find the object, it may be obstructed by some other object within the game. At the top of the viewport, there is a search bar. Searching for the object name will temporarily remove all other objects from the viewport except for the object you are looking for, pictured in Figure 2-3. You will now have an isolated environment to work on the sole object you have searched for. It is important for me to note that if you have created a reusable slice (which we will talk about in a later chapter), searching in this bar will isolate the viewport to all slices that share the same name.

Figure 2-3. *Searching for an object in the viewport will temporarily remove all other objects in order to have a more isolated workspace*

The last item we will talk about regarding the viewport is the "Toggle display helpers" tool, which lives in the far-right corner of the viewport whose icon is a question mark. This tool will come in handy for objects and entities that do not have materials or skins but still need to be acted upon. For example, a camera, enemy spawner, or a Lua script, to name a few. Pictured in Figure 2-4 on the left side is a shot of the viewport looking at an enemy spawner with a Lua script without the display helpers toggled on. On the right side is that same area of the viewport with the enemy spawner and Lua script *with the* display helpers toggled on. You can see how it would be helpful to have these helpers toggled on when you are wanting to manipulate objects without skins or materials, but you can also probably understand that always having display helpers toggled can muddle up your viewport rather quickly.

Figure 2-4. *The left side shows an area in the viewport without display helpers toggled on, while the right side shows the same area within the viewport with display helpers toggled on. We can now see there is an object in this spot, but we can also gather that there will be many non-skinned objects that can clutter the viewport if display helpers are constantly toggled on.*

Snapping Panes

On the left side of every window, tool, editor, toolbar, etc., in Amazon Lumberyard, there are three vertical dots. Holding down left-click will allow you to unsnap the pane (if it is already snapped) and either move it to its own window or snap it to a different area within the editor. While holding down left-click on the three vertical dots, drag the pane to an area where you would like to drop it, and you will see white bars on the top, bottom, left, and right of the area. Dragging the pane to one of these bars will turn the bar orange, as shown in the left photograph in Figure 2-5, and when you release the pane, it will be snapped to whichever bar was orange.

Alternatively, if you are like me, you would rather have your panes as "Tabs" rather than see everything all at once. While holding down left-click and dragging your pane, in the middle of the area you drag the pane over, you will see what looks like a folder with three tabs, as shown in the right photograph in Figure 2-5. Drag the pane to that icon until it turns orange, then let go. Your pane will now be a tab option within the area you have snapped it to.

This is a feature that makes Amazon Lumberyard such a nice tool to work with, because you can customize the editor yourself to suit your needs, wants, and preferences. You should feel comfortable customizing your workspace. Do not worry about ending up with a final product that seems unmanageable, as at any time you can reset the Lumberyard Editor to use the default layout. This will restore your windows, tools, and editors to the default view that you will see when opening the editor for the first time. In order to reset the workspace to the default view configuration, go to the menu bar at the top of the editor, select "View," then "Layouts," then "Restore Default Layout."

Figure 2-5. *The left side shows the Asset Browser pane being snapped to the right side of the area currently completely occupied by the Entity Outliner. It should be noted you also have the option of snapping this pane to the top, left, or bottom of this area as well. The right side shows the Asset Browser pane being snapped as a "tab" to the area currently occupied by the Entity Outliner.*

Introduction to the Asset Browser

The two panes that will be used the most in your game development with Amazon Lumberyard career are the Asset Browser window and the Entity Outliner window. While they are two different panes, they will frequently get used together. Because the Entity Outliner window will take further explanation when we discuss entities and slices, we will talk about it in a future chapter.

First, we are going to talk about the Asset Browser. The Asset Browser shows all your project assets in a source folder and file view to allow for ease of access and interaction with these assets. By default, the Asset Browser is typically open and snapped to the left side of your Editor workspace; however, if it is not, press Alt+T and select "Asset Browser" from the drop-down list. Alternatively, go to the menu bar, click "Tools," and select "Asset Browser" from the drop-down list.

The Asset Browser will show you all files and folders contained within your Asset Processor Platform configuration file located at `C:\Amazon\<LumberyardVersion>\dev\AssetProcessorPlatformConfig.ini`. You should not have to make many changes to this file for the purposes of this text, as we will be utilizing gems and assets that come with the engine which are included in this file by default. If there are changes you need to make due to adding your own assets that you have either created or purchased online, you can edit the file in your text editor of choice, and the instructions are detailed within the file itself as comments.

In the Asset Browser window, files that are usable within the Lumberyard Editor will appear in white text, while non-usable files such as .exe executables or .zip files will appear in gray, as the editor will not process these file types. There are certain file types that will contain products that make up the file, and the Asset Browser will therefore display these asset files with their products shown as children. For example, Filmbox files (`.fbx`) can contain animations, meshes, actor files and more as shown in Figure 2-6.

Figure 2-6. *The Asset Browser will display assets along with any product files that make up that asset*

One useful feature you can utilize when trying to locate an asset within the Asset Browser is the filter feature. The first, most obvious way to filter assets would be to search for them directly by name using the search bar in the tool's window. This will likely be the most common way of filtering out specific assets and files you need; however, there will be other times when you do not know the asset by name, but you do know the type. Lucky for you, the Asset Browser has a filter by asset type feature that can be used either stand-alone or in tandem with the search-by-name function. On the far right-hand side of the search bar on the Asset Browser window, there will be a funnel icon. When you click the icon, you have the option to filter what appears in the Asset Browser by the asset type, as shown in Figure 2-7.

Figure 2-7. *The filter by asset type tool is a handy way to display only assets of a certain type within the Asset Browser window*

Right-clicking assets in the Asset Browser will display a context menu that will give you some common options such as "Open in Explorer," "Copy Path to Clipboard," and "Copy Name to Clipboard" to name a few. These context menu options will change depending on the type of file you have selected. For example, right-clicking a .lua script file will present you with the option to open the script file within the Lumberyard LUA Editor. If you have source control such as Git, SVN, TFS, or some other version control software enabled on your project or on assets within the project, right-clicking the file in the Asset Browser will bring up a dialog with options related to source control, such as "Check Out," "Undo Check Out," "Get Latest Version," and "Add To Source Control" for files that have not yet been added to your repository.

Next, let's look at a few common buttons we will be using throughout the process of creating our game. We will start by going over buttons in the toolbar. The Lumberyard Editor provides a toolbar that makes various tools and features within the software easily accessible to the user. By default, the toolbar is docked at the top of the editor and includes all sub-toolbars, the EditMode toolbar, the Object toolbar, and the Editors toolbar. You can drag toolbars to dock them vertically on the edges of the editor, dock them to the bottom of the editor, or undock them completely, as they are fully customizable. Because they are customizable, note that it is possible to hide or show any sub-toolbars at any point in time by right-clicking the menu bar and selecting the toolbar you would like to hide or show. This is also how you can choose which views or modes to display.

Navigating the EditMode Toolbar

To begin, we will start by going over buttons on the "EditMode Toolbar," shown in Figure 2-8.

Figure 2-8. *The EditMode toolbar contains features that will make viewport navigation much simpler, as well as entity-sizing, placement, running the game, and general level editing tools*

From left to right, the first two buttons (A and B) do similar things. The first reverts the last command the user has input into the editor. Think of this as an undo button. Similarly, the second button will apply the last command, so if the user decided to undo something, they would click the first button, and if they changed their mind, they can click the second button to reapply the last command.

The next two buttons also perform similar actions, but we will not be using these actions in this book, so I will go over them very briefly. When an object is selected, you can click the first button (C), to begin linking that object to another. When you click another object, the object initially selected and the recently selected objects will be linked together. In order to break this link, or unlink the two objects, you can click the second button (D) while having the object selected.

The next five buttons are the translation tools. These are the tools that will likely be used the most throughout this entire project, so we need to be familiar and comfortable with using them. The first, (E), is the "Select" tool. This is selected by default, and when clicking an object or entity in the viewport, it will simply select the entity or object and put its information in the entity inspector, which we will talk about later in the chapter. The next button, (F), is the move tool. Moving objects and entities in Amazon lumberyard is not as simple as clicking and dragging them. The move tool will give us three arrows: one following the x-axis, one following the y-axis, and the last following the z-axis. Selecting one of these arrows *then* dragging will allow us to move that object along which ever axis' arrow we have selected.

The next button, (G), is the rotate tool. This tool provides a handy way to rotate objects in the viewport around any axis you want without accidentally rotating around another. When selected, you will be given three circles, each whose centers are the x-, y-, and z-axes. When holding down the red circle, you can rotate the object around the x-axis; when holding down the blue circle, you can rotate the object around the z-axis; and when holding down the green circle, you can rotate around the y-axis. You are also given a white circle that encompasses all of these, which allows you to rotate the axes themselves. The next translation tool, button (H), is the scale tool. When the scale tool is selected, clicking an object in the viewport will show you the x-, y-, and z-axes of the object with boxes at the ends of the axes. While holding the box, you can drag your mouse along the whichever axis the box belongs to in order to expand or contract the object along that axis. The final tool in the translation tool group, button (I), is the "Select Terrain" tool. We will be talking about terrain extensively in another chapter, so for now – just know that the Select Terrain tool is used to select or rotate terrain within the editor's viewport.

The next button (J) is another very important button in our game creation process. It is the "Play Game" button, and it will allow us to do exactly that. There is nothing better than working on a new object or script in our game, clicking that button, and getting to play with it. Just know that once this button is clicked, your mouse will no longer be usable in the Lumberyard Editor, as it will be constrained to the viewport window where the game will be in play mode. To exit the game and free up your mouse and keyboard, press the "Esc" button on your keyboard.

The next item on the EditMode toolbar (K) is another item we will not be using. It is a drop-down list that allows you to change the reference coordinate system between view, local, parent, world, and a custom coordinate system that you can set up.

Items (L), (M), (N), and (O) all do similar things and will change automatically when using any of the five translation tools we talked about earlier. Selecting (L) will allows you to specify the axis constraint to lock to the x-axis. For example, if you were to move an object using the translation move tool (F), clicking the x-axis arrow to move the object will automatically select the "Constrain to x-axis" tool. Similarly, (M) and (N) will allow you to specify the axis constraint to lock to the y- and z-axes, respectively. Button (O) sets the axis constraint to lock to the XY plane. Because these will automatically be selected when using other tools, we do not need to worry much about knowing when to select each of these.

The last set of tools on the EditMode toolbar (P), (Q), (R), (S), and (T) are called the "Object Placement tools." These tools will be used when placing new objects and entities into the viewport, selecting their locations within your game, and will be a tremendous help to you when moving them around.

Navigating the Object Toolbar

The next toolbar we will be looking at is the "Object toolbar," pictured in Figure 2-9, and it includes a myriad of tools for object manipulation as well as object alignment within the viewport.

Figure 2-9. *The Object toolbar contains features and tools that allow you to manipulate and align game objects with ease*

Most of the buttons in the Object toolbar will be grayed out and un-selectable unless there is an object or entity selected in the Entity Outliner window, which we discussed more in depth earlier in the chapter. That is because the functionality of these tools relies on manipulating and aligning objects, so if there is no entity or object selected, the tool will have no parameters to act on.

The first button on the Object toolbar, button (A), is the "Go to selected object" button. When you have an object or entity selected in the Entity Outliner window and click the "Go to selected object" button, the viewport will center the selected object within the view. As your game grows, this button will become increasingly important, as your game will typically contain many objects as work on your project progresses.

The next button (B), the "Align to object" button, will align the selection to an object by having a source object chosen in the Entity Outliner window, selecting the tool from the Object toolbar, and then clicking the target object to align with. The next tool is also an alignment tool; however, instead of aligning one object to another, button (C), the "Align to grid" tool will snap the object to the grid in the viewport. Because the transform tools will allow you to move objects anywhere in the viewport, games that require objects to be aligned or require symmetry can be difficult without the "Align to grid" tool. In order to use the "Align to grid" tool, you will need to have an object selected in the Entity Outliner window already, and upon clicking the button in the toolbar, the object will snap to the grid.

The fourth button on the Object toolbar, button (D), is the "Set object height" button, which is self-explanatory. When an object is selected in the Entity Outliner window, click the "Set object height" button, and a small window will pop out with an input field that allows you to give the selected object a numeric height, positive or negative. An object with a negative height will be placed below the terrain.

Button (E) is a little bit trickier to use. This is the "Align object to surface" button. To use this tool, select an object in the Entity Outliner window, click the "Align object to surface" button in the Object toolbar, and hold down the Ctrl button on your keyboard while moving your mouse in the viewport. The object will move along the terrain surface, even in places where the terrain forms hills or dips – the object will follow.

Buttons (F) and (G) are similar in functionality. When an object is selected in the Entity Outliner window, if the selected object is not already locked, clicking button (F), the "Lock Selection" button, will lock the object, making in incapable of being moved, scaled, or rotated. If the selected object is already locked, clicking button (F) will unlock the object, re-enabling transformation capabilities. Button (G), the "Unlock All" tool, will unlock all locked objects simultaneously.

The final button on the Object toolbar, button (H), is the "Vertex Snapping" tool. When this tool is selected, vertices on object are displayed in purple. If you click and hold one of these purple vertices, you can drag it to another purple vertex on a different object in order to snap two objects together at any two vertices between the objects.

Navigating the Editors Toolbar

The last toolbar we will tour will be one that we will not frequently use throughout this project; however, I still feel it is necessary to be introduced to it for future projects. The "Editors toolbar," shown in Figure 2-10, contains buttons that open a variety of different editors that Amazon Lumberyard offers, including the Terrain Editor, User Interface Editor, and Time of Day Editors, to name a few.

Figure 2-10.   *The Editors toolbar allows you to access various editor tools*

Because the Editors toolbar opens various editor tools within Amazon Lumberyard, you will likely have to flip back to Figure 2-10 every so often to refer to which button I am discussing, as they do not have quite as simple of functionality as the Object toolbar or the EditMode toolbars do.

The first in the fairly short list of editors on the toolbar, button (A), will open the Material Editor, shown in Figure 2-11, which is the principal tool that will be used to create materials, set opacity and lighting effects for material objects, set shader parameters, and more advanced functionality that we will not cover in this book.

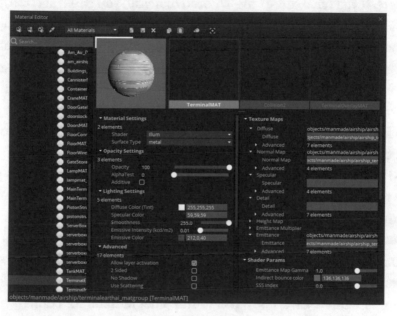

Figure 2-11. *Along with creating materials, the Material Editor allows you to set many advanced properties on object materials such as texture mapping, shader parameters, tessellation, and more*

Because there is so much functionality within this editor, I will not be discussing each button contained within it; however, I will go over some useful tools it is comprised of and some tools that you will perhaps use early on in your game development journey. As you become more familiar with game development throughout the course of this book and onward, I encourage you to come back to this editor as well as all future editor panes we will look at and experiment with the myriad of options and capabilities they offer.

If we look in the far-left pane of the editor, you can see a list of all available materials that you have loaded into your project. Selecting one of these listed materials will load the object into the Material Editor that will then allow you to edit its properties. Some of the common things you would edit here would be things like the opacity of the material; for example, if you have some blue-colored material, you could set the opacity to 50% or so to make a hologram style object. Another group of settings you may frequently be editing here in the Material Editor is the "Lighting Settings." These tools allow you to have blank spots in your material emit light or color, and if you choose to utilize this capability, the Material Editor allows you to choose the emissive color as well as intensity and smoothness of that emission. Other common settings you may like to make changes to would be things like the shader and surface type of your material, and all the settings I have just been discussing can be changed in the two panes you see to the right of the list pane and underneath the material artwork within the Material Editor window.

Let's look at the toolbar, where there are some tools that will help us navigate within the Material Editor window itself. Specifically, let's look at the first five tools on the toolbar, as the rest of the buttons on the toolbar are more intuitive (save, copy, paste, and other familiar functions).

The first three buttons at the top of the Material Editor window will require that you have an object or multiple objects selected in the Entity Outliner window. The first button allows you to select a material from the menu and apply that material to all selected objects from the Entity Outliner. The next button will allow you to reset the material on the selected objects to the default material.

The fourth button on the Material Editor window toolbar, the button whose icon is an eyedropper, is the one that is likely the most useful tool on the toolbar. Before selecting this tool, be sure you have the Material Editor window moved enough so that you can still see your viewport in the background. Select the "Pick Material from Object" tool, then in your viewport, select an entity whose material you would like to edit the properties of. The Material Editor will then load the properties from the selected object into the window for tinkering.

The next item in the toolbar of the Material Editor window and the final item we will talk about is a drop-down that will change the list in the far-left pane of materials to edit. Options will include "All Materials," which will show you all possible materials you have loaded into your project, and "Used In Level," which will only show you materials that you have utilized thus far in the current level you have loaded. We will talk about projects in levels in a future chapter; just note that it may be best to select the "Used In Level" option when tinkering in the Material Editor window, as many of our materials may be similarly named, and we would not want to unconsciously edit a material in a different level that we assume may be the correct material from the current level.

Back to the Editors toolbar, click the icon of a running person, and this will Open the EMotion FX Animation Editor (B), shown in Figure 2-12.

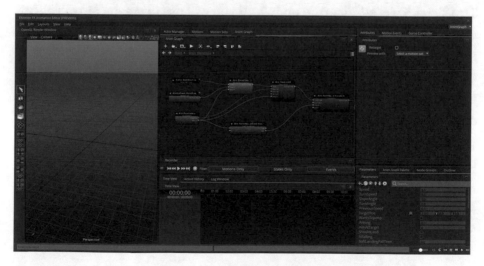

Figure 2-12. *The EMotion FX Animation Editor allows you to animate characters in Amazon Lumberyard, whether they be a character the player controls or an AI-driven character that interacts with the level*

Note   As of Amazon Lumberyard Version Number 1.17.0, the
EMotion FX Animation Editor, which from now on I will just call
the "Animation Editor," is in preview release, so it is subject to
change. Because of this, and the fact that we will not be using the
Animation Editor within this book, I will not be detailing how to use
the functionality of this tool. I will say, however, that in order to use
the Animation Editor to build a character, you will need to have used
Maya or some similar tool to link skinned models with an animation
skeleton and then import that character into the Animation Editor to
specify which animations you want your character to have.

The next button on the Editors toolbar, button (C), will open the
Track View editor which will help you add a certain level of polish and
professionalism to your game that will make it stand out among the rest.
The Track View editor is the main tool you will use to create, as well as set
and manage all cinematic sequences or animation events. The Track View
editor is used to control the entities, cameras and variables part of your
animations or cinematics, and create scripts to trigger animations. Similar
to the EMotion FX Animation Editor, the Track View editor has many
advanced functionalities you may learn to use as part of more complex
projects. The official Lumberyard documentation provides thorough
descriptions for these functionalities.

The next button on the Editors toolbar, button (D), will open the
Audio Controls editor which will allow you to create controls and make
connections between ATL Controls and middleware controls.

Note   ATL stands for Audio Transaction Layer, which is an abstraction layer that allows your game to communicate events and actions to the audio system. This will give you the ability to change quickly manipulate audio mappings without having to update the game's integration of controls.

The Audio Controls editor is split into three different areas. On the far left is your ATL Controls pane. This is a view of controls that exist within your project. The next, middle area called the "Inspector" pane will show all properties present on the control you have selected in the ATL Controls pane. The last area on the far right is a list of controls created in an audio middleware authoring application like Audiokinetic's Wwise.

The remaining buttons on the Editors toolbar will be covered in depth in future chapters. Buttons (E), (F), (H), and (I), the Terrain Editor, Terrain Texture Layers Editor, Time of Day Editor, and Sun Trajectory tool, respectively, will be discussed in detail in Chapter 4. Button (G), which opens the particle editor, will be discussed in detail in Chapter 9. Lastly, Button (J) opens the User Interface Editor, or UI Editor, which will be discussed in depth in Chapter 10.

Time-Saving Key Bindings

Before the computer mouse as we know it today was first brought to market in the 1960s, everything done on computers was done by keystrokes. There is something to be said about doing your work by keystroke alone, and in fact – many programmers prefer it. While we cannot develop games without the aide of a mouse, there are a few navigation tricks we can use by utilizing keystrokes only, as well as a few editors we can open. For that reason, I have built a table in Figure 2-13 of some of the most popular key bindings that I have found to be the

most useful to me personally while working in the Amazon Lumberyard
Editor. By no means is this a comprehensive list, as there are far more key
bindings than these. Note that many of the standard key combinations
will work in Amazon Lumberyard as well such as Ctrl+Z to undo, Ctrl+C to
copy, Ctrl+V to paste, and so on.

A	Moves the viewer left in the viewport
S	Moves the viewer backwards in the viewport
W	Moves the viewer forward in the viewport
D	Moves the viewer right in the viewport
Q	Moves the viewer up in the viewport
E	Moves the viewer down in the viewport
M	Opens the Material Editor, discussed earlier in the chapter
T	Opens the Track Editor, discussed earlier in the chapter
R	When an object is selected within the viewport or in the Entity Outliner window, pressing R will select the object's parent if one exists.
`	Opens the console window
Ctrl+O	Opens the "Open Level" dialog
Ctrl+S	Saves the current Level
Ctrl+G	Enters game mode, which will allow you to test the progress of the game thus far, similar to the "Play Game" button on the EditMode toolbar discussed earlier in the chapter.

Figure 2-13. *Keyboard shortcuts are a great way to stay productive
when the mouse is otherwise occupied*

You now know the ins and outs of the Amazon Lumberyard Editor and many of the tools associated with it. You have also been able to successfully open the Lumberyard Editor and know many workarounds and fixes for common problems when doing so.

In the next chapter, we will create our first project as well as our first level. We are going to discuss what gems are, how to enable them, how to build the game as well as the engine, and more.

CHAPTER 3

Creating Your First Project

We have installed the Lumberyard engine, Editor, Setup Assistant, and Project Configurator. We have also gone over various toolbars, tools, panes, and shortcuts within the Lumberyard Editor. Now that we covered the basic fundamentals to the Lumberyard engine, it is time to finally create something. In this chapter, all the fun begins. We are going to create our very first project and discuss how to use the Project Configurator in order to customize what components we have at our disposal. We are going to talk about compiling the project as well as the engine, how to create levels and how levels relate to projects as a whole.

Opening the Project Configurator

Installed alongside the Amazon Lumberyard Setup Assistant and Lumberyard Editor is the Lumberyard Project Configurator. Amazon Lumberyard is comprised of many different component projects that work in tandem to create the final project. This may feel different to you as a user, as typically when working with other programs, you can create a project, work in the project, save, and build the project all from a single window within the application. While this may take some time to get used to, do not worry – it all feels natural the more you work with the platform.

© Jaken Chandler Herman 2019
J. C. Herman, *Beginning Game Development with Amazon Lumberyard*,
https://doi.org/10.1007/978-1-4842-5073-0_3

Let's get started. We will start by opening the Project Configurator which, again, can be opened by taking two different routes. We are going to walk through both processes to opening the Project Configurator so that you have the ability to choose which one is your favorite on your own, and that will mostly depend on whether you are a command-line junkie or not.

The first method would be to either click the Windows icon in the bottom-left corner or press the Windows key on your keyboard in order to open the start menu. Type "Project Configurator" and click the purple icon that shows up. Alternatively, if you are running a version of Windows where the Cortana helper is on your taskbar, you can ask her to open it for you, or type "Project Configurator" in her search bar.

The next method of opening the Project Configurator is through the command line. Because I am used to using source control, compiling code and building projects from the command line so often, I tend to prefer using commands to navigating user interfaces. If that is not something you are interested in, skip to the next section of the book. Open Powershell by pressing the Windows key on your keyboard and the "X" button on your keyboard at the same time. This will open the Power User Tasks menu. Press "I" on your keyboard to open up Powershell. Navigate to the Amazon Lumberyard "dev" directory by running the command:

```
cd C:\Amazon\Lumberyard\1.17.0.0\dev
```

Keep in mind that if your instance of Amazon Lumberyard is installed on a drive other than your C: drive, you will need to modify that command a little bit. Similarly, if you have a different version of Amazon Lumberyard installed on your machine, you will need to replace the "1.17.0.0" portion of that command with the version number you have installed locally. Now, think back to Chapter 2. If your Lumberyard Editor opened *without* having to navigate to the "Bin64vc141" directory, then to open the Project Configurator, you will run the following command:

```
.\Bin64vc140\ProjectConfigurator.exe
```

And if you *did* have to navigate to the "Bin64vc141" directory, then you will open the Project Configurator by running the following command:

```
.\Bin64vc141\ProjectConfigurator.exe
```

It should not take long for the Project Configurator to open, and when it does, it will look like Figure 3-1.

Figure 3-1. *The user interface of the Project Configurator's main window is extremely simple, showing you all projects on your machine with buttons navigating to more advanced functionality*

Creating Your First Project

Now that we have successfully opened the Project Configurator, it is time to get to what this chapter is all about – creating our first project. There are two ways of creating a project in Amazon Lumberyard:

- Through the Project Configurator user interface tool

- Through the command-line tools provided by Amazon Lumberyard

Once again, we are going to walk through both methods. I would highly recommend, however, that even if you are planning to use the command-line interface, you read through the Project Configurator method, as there will be information contained within it about project templates. Another useful piece of information that will be contained within the Project Configurator section will be what the tools are doing in the background when a new project is being created.

Creating a Project Through the Project Configurator

Upon opening the Project Configurator, you will see small cards for each Amazon Lumberyard project you have on your machine. Note that because Amazon Lumberyard comes bundled with different starter projects, you should already have some sample projects listed here. Not shown in Figure 3-1 is a button in the very top-right corner of the Project Configurator that says, "Set as default," which we will discuss more in detail later.

For now, we are going to ignore these sample projects and begin learning the ins and outs of the Project Configurator by creating our very own first project. At the top of the Project Configurator next to the bold header that reads "Select a project" is a blue button that says, "Create new." Select the "Create new" button, and you will be greeted with two options – Default and Empty, as shown in Figure 3-2.

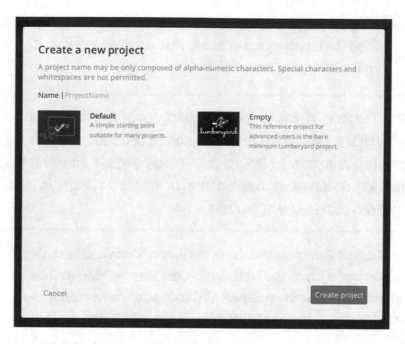

Figure 3-2. *These are your two options for creating a new project, Default, which includes many common components, and Empty which is a completely bare-bones project for advanced users*

The Empty Template has the bare minimum features that are required just to load and run a game project. This should only be selected by advanced users of Amazon Lumberyard who know exactly what gems to enable and what advanced settings to change to fit their needs. There are four features that come loaded on the Empty Template:

- CryLegacy, which enables the editor and launcher to load game projects that contain legacy code

- The Maestro gem which grants the user access to the use of cinematic features

- The LyShine gem which will provide the user with necessary access to the User Interface system within Amazon Lumberyard

- Legacy Game Interface, which will enable the launcher and the Lumberyard Editor to load a game project that contains legacy interface code

---

Note   "Legacy" is a fancy way of saying "outdated, but still in use." Anything related to computing can be considered legacy like hardware, programming languages, or tools that are either no long in production, no longer in maintenance, or simply no longer in business but are still being used in projects.

The Default Template builds on the Empty Template, meaning it comes bundled with all the features that the Empty Template has while having more gems enabled to provide basic game development features. The Default Template comes loaded with the following:

- Camera, which is massively important in your game development. This gem will provide a basic camera component for runtime rendering.

- Gestures, which allows gesture-based input for mobile devices or 2-in-1 devices that support gesture inputs like tap, hold, drag, swipe, and more.

- HttpRequestor, which will allow you to make HTTP and HTTPS requests from within your game.

- In-App Purchases, which will include the in-app purchasing APIs for iOS and Android mobile platforms.

- Physics Entities, which is a legacy gem, but provides you with the ability to simulate physical events like gravity, for example.

- Primitive Assets, which provides primitive objects that are already physics enabled.

- ChatPlay, which provides a framework to create game interactions between spectators and broadcasters on the popular video streaming platform Twitch. This gem includes support for polls, surveys, and chat commands.

- Amazon GameLift, which makes it easier for you to use Amazon GameLift in Lumberyard. GameLift is an AWS service that provides many support methods for multiplayer games.

- Cloud Canvas, which provides visual scripting to AWS services like DynamoDB, Lambda, Cognito, SQS, and more AWS services.

- Input Management Framework is an important gem if you want to have multiple input methods like different gamepads and keyboard layouts. This gem provides a framework for managing such cross-platform game inputs.

- PBS Reference Materials, which includes a set of shading reference materials and texture assets.

- All four of the components that are preloaded on the Empty Template.

When a project is created using the Default Template, the project will also include a simple level for experimentation which will have a camera, a single light source, and primitive objects. Because we would like a good starting point for our game, let us select the "Default" option in the "Create new project" window, name the project "MyFirstGame," and click the blue "Create project" button in the bottom-right corner of the window. The process of creating a new project takes a bit of time, so sit back and relax while Amazon Lumberyard gets your project ready.

Why does it take so long? What is it doing? When a new project is created in the Project Configurator using the Default Template, multiple things are happening. The Project Configurator will create a new project using the `DefaultTemplate`, which is in the directory:

`\dev\ProjectTemplates\DefaultTemplate`

Everything in the template's code directory, located at

`\dev\ProjectTemplates\DefaultTemplate\code\DefaultTemplate`

will be copied into your new project's code directory, located at

`\dev\code\MyFirstGame`

All other contents of the template folder that are not code components, located in

`\dev\ProjectTemplates\DefaultTemplate`

will be copied into your new project's directory, located in

`\dev\MyFirstGame`

The `DefaultTemplate` references are replaced in both new `MyFirstGame` directories with the name of the new project, including all file names and contents. Note that in all the preceding directories, assume you are already in your Lumberyard versions directory, which we navigated to earlier at `C:\Amazon\Lumberyard\<lumberyard_version>`.

Creating a Project Through the CLI

Another method we can use to create projects is, of course, via the command-line interface. When projects are created through the command-line interface, the template they are generated from is the Default Template. To create a project through the command line, open your Powershell either by searching for it in the start menu or by using the key-combination Windows key + "X," then "I." Change directories to your Lumberyard dev directory, as we have done earlier in the chapter:

```
cd C:\Amazon\Lumberyard\<lumberyard_Version>\dev
```

Now change directories to whichever Bin64vc14X folder that has been working for you (Bin64vc140 for Visual Studio 2015, Bin64vc141 for Visual Studio 2017+):

```
cd Bin64vc14X
```

This folder is, of course, where the Lumberyard Editor executable file is found, but it is also home to an executable called lmbr, which handles a myriad of project tasks such as creating projects; setting projects as active (as we will see later); creating, enabling, and disabling gems; and more.

Note   Gems are more easily thought of as "plugins." A gem is a package that contains game assets or code that you can use in your project. When creating a new project, you can select which gems you would like to include and which you would like to exclude. This allows you to create gems that are reusable from project to project while still providing the ability to pick and choose what aspects of the project you feel as if you can leave behind.

Enter the following command to create your project, which we will name "MyFirstProject" to be consistent with the name we used in the project configurator:

```
.\lmbr projects create MyFirstProject
```

Once you get a response from your command line that says "Project 'MyFirstProject' successfully created," you are done, as your project has been created.

Setting Default Projects

Once you have a project created, you will need to set it as the default project in order to open it. When I first began working with Amazon Lumberyard, this came as a bit of a surprise to me, as most other software allows you to simply "Open [a different] project" from the File menu in the menu bar. Amazon Lumberyard does not offer this option; rather it offers a "Switch Project" option in the File menu which will open the Project Configurator and this closes the editor as the two cannot be running simultaneously. Setting a project as the default project in the Project Configurator is as simple as clicking the blue "Set as default" button in the top-right corner of the Project Configurator while having the project's card selected, as shown in Figure 3-3.

Figure 3-3. *These are your two options for creating a new project, Default, which includes many common components, and Empty which is a completely bare-bones project for advanced users*

Of course, this section would not be complete without detailing how to set the project as the default project via the command-line interface. Change your directory to the Bin64vc14X directory by using the process outlined in the "Create a Project through the CLI" subsection earlier in the chapter, then run the following command:

```
.\lmbr projects set-active MyFirstGame
```

Once you have run the command, you will not get a response back from your command line unless it errored out, which should only happen if your command had a typo. Your project will now be set to the default project. From this point on, any time you attempt to open the Amazon Lumberyard Editor, this will be the project that is loaded. At any point in time, if you would like to change your default project to another, simply repeat the preceding steps replacing "MyFirstGame" with the name of the game project you would like to be set as the default.

Gems

As previously mentioned, gems are like plugins you can enable or disable on your project to take reusable code and assets from one project and implement them in another. If you look back at Figure 3-1 earlier in the chapter, you may be able to tell that options to enable gems or view advanced settings are not available to all projects in the Project Configurator. In order to enable or disable gems and view advanced settings for a project, that project must be selected in order to make changes. This, however, does *not* mean that when a project is selected in the Project Configurator, it is now the default project; it simply means that you are loading the gems and settings currently enabled on that project.

Enabling Gems

Enabling gems through the Project Configurator User Interface is the easiest method, so let us explore this method first. To begin, select the project you would like to enable gems on. For the purposes of this text, we will continue with "MyFirstGame." From here, you will see the option to enable gems on this project, as shown in Figure 3-4. Click this button, and a window will pop up allowing you to select or deselect gems from your project.

Figure 3-4. *The easiest way to enable and disable gems is through the Project Configurator User Interface tool*

There is a search bar in the top-right corner of this window if you know the name of the gem you want to change the status of. If you are unsure of the gem's name or you are just discovering the other available gems, however, you can scroll through the list available to you in the center of the window. Each gem has its own row with three important pieces of information on it. First, at the far left of each gem row, there is a checkbox. If the checkbox is selected, this gem is already enabled on your project. If the checkbox is unselected, this gem has not been enabled. The middle column of each gem row is the gem artwork and description, telling you exactly what the gem provides for your project. To the right, the last column of each gem row lists the dependencies required for this gem to run properly. If a gem is selected that has dependencies, you will also need to ensure that you enable the dependency gems as well.

For our project, most of the gems necessary will already be enabled because we opted to use the Default Project template when creating our project. There is, however, one gem we would like to enable that will give us artwork and character models provided by Amazon Lumberyard to get started. Search in the gem window "Starter Game Gem," enable it, and click the blue "Save" button in the top-right corner of the window.

Another method of enabling gems is through the command line, and there are many different commands to create gems and modify a project's use of gems. To run these commands, we will need to be in either the Bin64vc140 or Bin64vc141 directory (depending on which version of Visual Studio you have enabled). Navigate to this directory by using the following

command, replacing <Bin_Version> with whichever directory you have
had success with in earlier sections of this book:

```
Amazon\Lumberyard\<Lumberyard_Version>\dev\<Bin_Version>
```

From this directory, we can run many different commands to modify
gem status on our project. In order to see a list of gems available for your
use, run the command:

```
.\lmbr gems list
```

If you would like to see which gems are already installed or enabled on
a specified project, you can modify this command by adding the -project
flag, followed by the name of the project you would like to see the list of
gems for. For our game, "MyFirstGame," that command would be the
following:

```
.\lmbr gems list -project MyFirstGame
```

To enable gems on your project via the command line, you replace
"list" in the preceding commands with "enable," followed by the project
name to enable the gem on, then followed by the gem name that you
would like to enable. This will install the latest version of the named gem
on the named project:

```
.\lmbr gems enable MyFirstGame <Gem_Name>
```

As stated earlier in the chapter, for our "MyFirstGame" project, most
of the necessary gems will be enabled already due to our choice of using
the Default Project template when creating our project; therefore, we only
need to enable the "Starter Game Gem" provided by Amazon Lumberyard
to get started. Run the following command to enable the Starter Game
Gem in our project:

```
.\lmbr gems enable MyFirstGame StarterGameGem
```

You should see confirmation text in your command-line window that says something along the lines of "Successfully enabled Gem StarterGameGem." You will also notice that running this command will enable all dependent gems required by the Starter Game Gem as well, such as LmbrCentral and EMotionFX.

There may come a time where you want to enable a specific version of a gem rather than enabling the latest version by default. This can be done by modifying the enable command by adding the -version flag, followed by the version you would like to enable, like so:

```
.\lmbr gems enable <Project_Name> <Gem_Name> -version <Version_Number>
```

Disabling a gem on a project by means of the command line is very similar to enabling gems. In order to disable a given gem on a project, you would run the following command:

```
.\lmbr gems disable <Project_Name> <Gem_Name>
```

The gem you named will be disabled from on the project you named, but it should be mentioned that the dependencies that were enabled to support the newly disabled gem will *not* be disabled by running the preceding command. If you are confident that the dependencies were only used for the gem you are disabling, you can disable dependencies alongside gems by modifying the preceding command, adding the -disable-deps flag, like so:

```
.\lmbr gems disable <Project_Name> <Gem_Name> -disable-deps
```

When gems are enabled or disabled within a game project, in the background, the Project Configurator updates the list of enabled gems that is maintained in a JSON file called gems.json located in the game's project directory:

```
Amazon\Lumberyard\<Lumberyard_Version>\dev\<Game_Project_Name>
```

Enabling or disabling gems will also update the Game.xml and Editor.xml files, which tell Amazon Lumberyard to load the required DLL files for the gems that you have enabled in the Project Configurator, which are in the directory:

```
Amazon\Lumberyard\<Lumberyard_Version>\dev\<Game_Project_Name>\Config
```

Note   JSON stands for "JavaScript Object Notation," which is a type of file used to store data with key-value pairs. It is very easy to read these files as humans, but more importantly, it is very easy for machines to generate and parse these files.

XML stands for "eXtensible Markup Language," which is a tool used for storing and transporting data that is both software and hardware independent. Similar to HTML, XML is a markup language. The difference between XML and HTML is that XML was designed to carry data, while HTML was designed to display data. XML tags do not need to be predefined, which is why it is a great tool to use for multiple different applications with differing use cases.

Because these background files get updated when a change is made to your project, any time you make changes to gem statuses or advanced settings, you will need to rebuild your game via the command line before opening the Lumberyard Editor. Failing to build the game after changes have been made to gems could result in errors on the startup of the editor. As a safety precaution, I typically also recommend rebuilding the engine and the game every time a change is made outside of the editor just to ensure that nothing goes wrong when you are ready to begin working.

At the time of writing this book, there is only one method for building your game project, and that is through the command line by running the Lmbr.exe file. If you have been following the user interface methods of performing actions throughout this book and find the command line daunting – fear not, this is a very simple process. The first thing we will need to do open up Powershell by pressing the Windows key + X to open the Power User Tasks menu, then press "I." The next task we will perform will be to navigate to our version of Amazon Lumberyard's dev directory which we have done many times before by running the command:

```
cd C:\Amazon\Lumberyard\<Lumberyard_Verion>\dev
```

Once we are in the Lumberyard dev directory, we will need to first configure the project by running the following command:

```
.\lmbr_waf configure
```

When the project configuration has completed, we will run the lmbr_waf command again, this time replacing "configure" with the build command. In the following, I will be running the command for Visual Studio 2017. If you have a different version of Visual Studio installed on your machine, replace "2017" in the following command with the correct year version you have installed:

```
.\lmbr_waf build_win_x64_vs2017_profile -p game
```

Earlier I mentioned that I would advise you to build both the game and the engine when project changes are made. The preceding command will only handle the building of the game. To build the engine alongside building the game, run the following command:

```
.\lmbr_waf build_win_x64_vs2017_profile -p game_and_engine
```

Depending on your last build, these commands may take quite a while to run.

Creating Gems

Because there will be times that you would like to reuse code snippets or assets that you have created from one project to another, we need to go over how to package those components into a gem for reusability.

First, think of a good name for your gem. For this example, we will use the name "MyNewGem." Then, in whichever Bin64vc140 or Bin64vc141 directory that has been allowing you success, run the following command:

```
.\lmbr gems create MyNewGem
```

A new gem folder will be created within the Amazon\<Version>\dev\ Gems directory, titled "MyNewGem." If you would like the gem folder name to be different than that of the gem's name, you can modify the preceding command by adding on the -out-folder flag, followed by the directory name you would like to use instead:

```
.\lmbr gems create MyNewGem -out-folder gems\<some_other_name>
```

If you would like to specify the version number of the gem you are creating, you can also add the -version flag to the command. Keep in mind version numbers must be in three parts, such as version 1.0.0 instead of version 1.0. To create a gem with a specified version number, run the following command, replacing <Version_Number> with whichever version of the gem you are creating:

```
.\lmbr gems create MyNewGem -version <Version_Number>
```

Now when you navigate to the directory of this newly created gem, you will see two folders: Assets and Code. Any reusable assets you have can be copied into the assets folder, and any reusable code you have can be copied into the code folder. You can also add a PNG image file called "MyNewGem_gem.png" into the gem directory to have artwork associated with your gem when it is viewed through the Project Configurator User Interface.

Advanced Project Settings

There are many settings that can be changed in a project by way of the advanced project settings window, also called the System Entity Editor. To open the System Entity Editor, navigate to the Project Configurator, select a project, and select the option "Advanced Settings," shown in Figure 3-5.

Figure 3-5. *Change advanced settings on both your game as well as the editor from the System Entity Editor, accessible from the Project Configurator User Interface*

When the System Entity Editor launches, you will see the main interface has two tabs – the System Entity tab as well as the Memory Settings tab. On the left side of Figure 3-6, you will see what the System Entity tab looks like, and on the right side of Figure 3-6, you will see what the Memory Settings tab looks like.

By default, when the System Entity Editor launches, the System Entity tab will be the selected tab, meaning the default view will be the System Entity view.

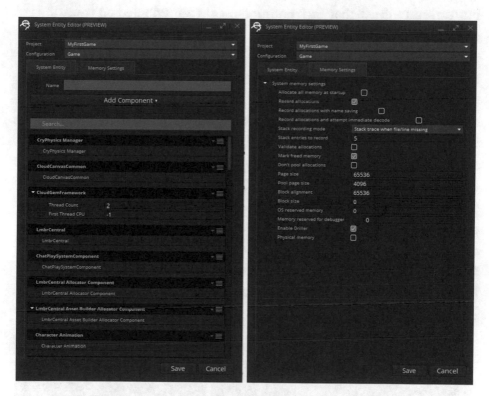

Figure 3-6. *The two settings tabs available in the System Entity Editor. On the left, the System Entity tab, and on the right, the Memory Settings Tab.*

In the top of the System Entity tab, you will see two drop-down menus. The first allows you to decide which game project you are changing settings on, while the second selects the configuration, either game or editor, whose settings will be changed. Then, you will see the tabs that provide you the option to switch between viewing the System Entity window and the Memory Settings window. Below these tabs is where the real configuration begins. To add a settings component, click the button that reads "Add Component." This will provide a list of available components alongside a search bar that allows you to quickly find the specific component you are looking for. Below the "Add Component" button, you will see that each component already enabled on your project will have its own card. A card with no inputs means there are no available customizations you can make to a component, while a card with inputs will allow you to change the given input's settings. For example, in Figure 3-6, the "CryPhysics Manager" has no available settings to change, while the "CloudGemFramework" has inputs that will allow you to configure the "Thread Count" as well as the "First Thread CPU" options.

For our game, the only changes we will make to the settings will be on the Input System component. In the System Entity Editor window on the System Entity tab, search "Input System." In the Input System card, we will deselect "Motion," "Touch," and "Virtual Keyboard," shown in Figure 3-7, as our game will only support the Keyboard and Mouse input devices. Once you have finished this book, if you would like to extend your game for mobile devices, feel free to come back to this System Entity Editor and re-enable the "Touch" input system.

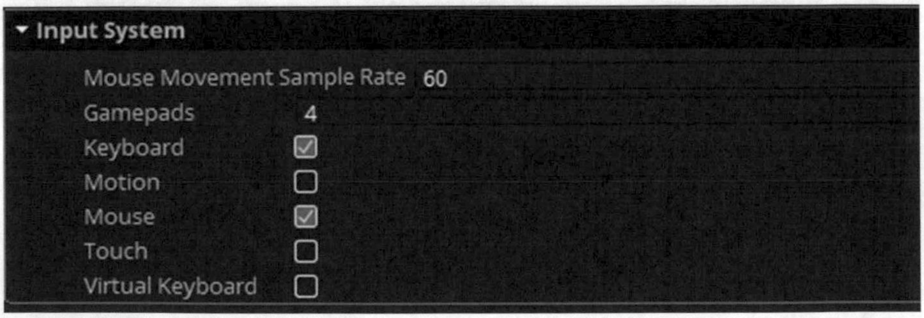

Figure 3-7. *For the purposes of this text, we only need to have the Keyboard and Mouse option selected for the "Input System" component*

We will opt to not make any changes to the Memory Settings of the project, as the default settings are typically sufficient for most projects. Click the gray "Save" button in the bottom right-hand corner of the System Entity Editor window to save our changes.

Levels

At this point, we have created a new project, changed advanced settings to suit our needs, enabled gems that will help us get started, and set the project as the default project. Now, it's time to add our first level. Before we do that, allow me to detail what a level is and how it differs from a project.

Level files are the system in which Amazon Lumberyard organizes the content of your games. Level files will contain all scripts, terrain changes, and support files that hold game data required for the level to run in the game. Per game, there will only be one project, but there will be many levels. Levels do not require a "default" setting to open and change like projects do. Unlike most other functions in Amazon Lumberyard, levels are only created from the user interface without a command-line counterpart and are created through the Lumberyard Editor rather than through their own configurator or setup assistant.

Creating a New Level

To begin, we first need to open the Amazon Lumberyard following the steps laid out in Chapter 2 of this book. When the editor opens, you will be greeted with a welcome window with the options "New Level" and "Open Level." Select the option "New Level" to create your first level. If you have already closed the welcome window, however, there are still two other ways you can create a level.

The first, go to the main menu at the top of the screen, and select "File," then "New Level." The second, use the keyboard combination option by pressing Ctrl+N simultaneously. Figure 3-8 shows the "New Level Creation Window," which contains five options.

Figure 3-8. *The New Level Creation Window is a very simple dialog to navigate through*

The first option is the level name input field. Level names cannot use spaces or any special characters aside from hyphens (-) and underscores (_). Alphanumeric characters are the accepted characters for level names. For our project, we will name our level "Level_1." Type this into the "Name" field now.

The next option allows you to select the folder the level is created in. By default, Amazon Lumberyard will create the level file within the project directory, in this case:

```
C:\Amazon\<Lumberyard_Version>\dev\MyFirstGame\Levels\<Level_Name>
```

While you have the privilege to change this directory, I will opt to leave the folder location as the default location.

The third option when creating a new level is a checkbox that sets the status for the "Use Terrain" property. Not all games will use terrain, so this option along with the next two options can be disabled. Our game, however, will have terrain, so we need to ensure that this checkbox is selected.

The fourth option allows you to change the terrain's heightmap resolution. As we will see in Chapter 4, Amazon Lumberyard provides us with some sample heightmaps with the resolution of 512x512 pixels. While heightmaps can be generated easily for any heightmap resolution setting, let's change this value to 512x512 so we can use the artwork provided to us by the engine.

The fifth and final option to change when creating a level is the "Meters Per Texel" option. This sounds a bit more daunting than it really is and is more easily explained by simply tinkering around with the Terrain Editor (which we will explore in Chapter 4). Meters per texel is the distance between to vertices on the game grid, in meters. If the meters per texel value is set to 8, for example, that would mean there is a grid point every 8 meters. Larger meters per texel values will create a larger terrain; however, the detail quality will decrease for the same heightmap resolution. In other words, "Terrain Size" is determined by multiplying the meters per texel by the heightmap resolution. For our purposes, let us select 1 meter per texel (if not already set by default), and we can see in the helper text below the meters per texel drop-down that our Terrain Size will be 512 x 512 meters.

Click the gray "OK" button in the bottom right-hand corner of the "New Level" window to save our changes. You will now be greeted with a window that allows you to set the Texture Dimensions as shown in Figure 3-9. This window will calculate texels per meter by dividing the selected Texture Dimensions by the Terrain Size set in the "New Level" creation window. Select the option 4096 x 4096 which will provide us with 8 texels per meter, and click the gray "OK" button in the bottom right-hand corner of the screen.

Figure 3-9. *Selecting a Terrain Texture Dimension will calculate the Texels per meter your project will use by dividing the selected Texture Dimensions by the Terrain Size*

Congratulations! You have just created your first level. You will now have an empty level with a flat terrain in your level file, as shown in your viewport.

Deleting a Level

Suppose you have created a level that you feel no longer has a place in your game. How do you get rid of this level entirely? While there is no option through the editor to remove the level, we can delete levels by going through the file system. We have two options for doing this.

The first method for deleting a level relies on the command line. Open Powershell by using the key-combination Windows key + X, then "I." Navigate to your levels directory by running the following command:

```
cd C:\Amazon\<Lumberyard_Version>\dev\<Game_Name>\Levels\
```

To see the list of levels you have the option of deleting, you can run the command `ls` in Powershell or `dir` in command line. Now, to delete the level, just run the following command, replacing <Level_Name> with the name of the level you would like to delete:

```
rm <Level_Name>
```

You will likely get a warning saying that the level has children and the recurse parameter was not specified. Because we want to remove the level as well as all of the children associated with it, we can type "A" and press "Enter" in order to agree to deleting all of the named level's children. At this point if you are unaware of what children are, do not worry – we will talk about parent-child entity relationships in Chapter 5.

The second method for deleting a level is a more user-interface friendly method. Open your File Explorer, and navigate to the directory:

```
C:\Amazon\<Lumberyard_Version>\dev\<Game_Name>\Levels\
```

Now, select the level you would like to delete and either select the "Home" tab and click the "Delete" option, signified by the red "X," or right-click the level folder and select the "Delete" option.

Changing Levels

To change the level currently loaded in the editor, there are two options. The first, navigate to the menu bar at the top of the screen and select "File," followed by "Open Level…." You will now see a window with a list of levels your project is associated with, as shown in Figure 3-10. The second method is to use the keyboard combination option by pressing Ctrl+O simultaneously to open the same window.

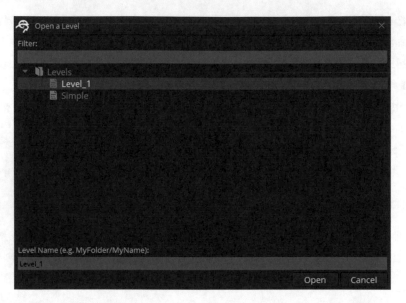

Figure 3-10. *The "Open a Level" window allows you to change the currently loaded level in the Lumberyard Editor*

As projects grow, the number of levels associated with that project will increase. Because of this, the "Open a Level" window provides a search bar that allows you to search for the level you would like to load by name.

Now that you have learned all about the basic components – projects, gems, and levels – we now know how to get started with the development of your first game. Chapter 4 will walk you through terrain development, which will give our game project a very polished, professional look.

CHAPTER 4

Terrain

This is the chapter where things begin to get fun. We are finally going to dig in, get our hands dirty, and work on creating the very first aspects of our game. Before we create a character entity and enemies and scripts, let us create a stunning terrain for them to interact with that will give our game a polished, professional look. In this chapter, we will discuss what a heightmap is, how to use them in Amazon Lumberyard, as well as how to create your own. We will talk about both textures and megatextures and focus on how they can be used to paint your terrain in such a way that will make them look realistic. We will go over how to give your terrain realistic depth and polish by adding vegetation while also discussing the downfalls of over-vegetating your game. We will also talk about sun patterns and setting the time of day.

As we go through this chapter, keep in mind I will merely be telling you how to create terrain, but as this is a creative aspect of the game rather than technical, I will not be detailing specifics on what vegetation to use, how high your mountains should be, or the time of day in which your game will be set. This will allow you to use your artistic capacity to create a game that is completely and truly your own, allowing you the imaginative freedom to explore the Lumberyard engine.

© Jaken Chandler Herman 2019
J. C. Herman, *Beginning Game Development with Amazon Lumberyard*,
https://doi.org/10.1007/978-1-4842-5073-0_4

Getting Started

To begin, open the project we created in Chapter 3 called "MyFirstGame" by opening the Lumberyard Editor using your preferred method described in Chapter 2. Remember that this project must be set as the default to be loaded into the editor. Once the Lumberyard Editor has loaded, select the "Level_1" level that was also created in Chapter 3. Terrain editing will be handled through the "Terrain Editor," which was briefly mentioned in Chapter 2. There are two ways to open the Terrain Editor.

The first and likely the easiest way to open the Terrain Editor is through the Editors toolbar. Select the "Terrain Editor" button, indicated by an icon with a mountain and a cloud on it, as pictured in Figure 4-1.

Figure 4-1. *Opening the Terrain Editor through the Editors toolbar is likely the easiest method of opening the tool, assuming the Editors toolbar is displayed in your editor window*

The next method of opening the Terrain Editor is to either navigate to the menu bar and click the "Tools" option or use the keyboard key-combination "Alt+T." Once the tools menu is showing, select the "Terrain Editor" option from the drop-down list. Depending on which version of Amazon Lumberyard you are running, this editor may already be enabled. The Terrain Editor will now be open, showing a flat heightmap, as shown in Figure 4-2.

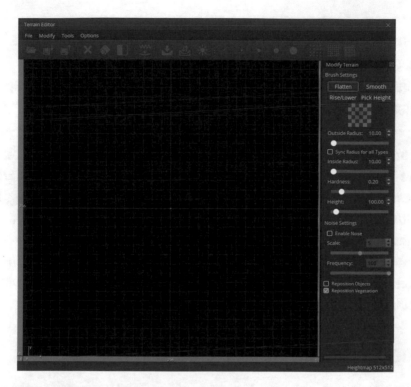

Figure 4-2. *The Terrain Editor allows you to create professional terrain for your game project*

Heightmaps

The first aspect of terrain editing we will discuss will be heightmaps. A heightmap, sometimes referred to as a heightfield in other applications, is a raster image that contains pixels which store elevation data for surfaces. The beauty of using heightmaps is that they are reusable from level to level, as once your heightmap is created, it can then be exported from one level, then imported to another. This will allow ease of continuity from level to level that both speeds up your development time and requires substantially less memory for the given level of detail provided.

Note   A raster image, also known as a bitmap, is a grid of pixels that compose an image. Think of a collection of multiple small squares, each with their own color that come together to make up a larger picture.

Heightmaps will always be black-and-white monochrome images, where black will signify no elevation, or flatness, and white will signify the highest elevation possible. Different shades of gray will, of course, signify elevations along some spectrum that are both lower than the highest possible elevation and higher than the lowest elevation. For example, a heightmap that is mostly black in color will result in a fairly flat terrain, whereas a brighter heightmap with very few or no black coloration will result in a very elevated, mountainous terrain.

Importing Heightmaps

Because Amazon Lumberyard comes packaged with a sample heightmap, I will walk you through how to import heightmaps into your game. Keep in mind, however, that it is not necessary that you follow along with these steps if you plan on creating your own heightmap which I will go over later in this section. To begin importing a premade heightmap from within the Terrain Editor, navigate to the menu bar and click "File" to display a drop-down, and from the options, select "Import Heightmap...." This will open a Windows Explorer window in your game's current directory. Navigate to the directory in Amazon\Lumberyard\<Lumberyard_Version>\dev\ StarterGame, then select "Textures" followed by "Heightmaps."

As you can see, there will be three options available to you: *AM_Terre_ HM_01, AM_Terre_HM_02,* and *FTUI_heightmap_Test*. From left to right, the far-left option, *AM_Terre_HM_01* is going to by far have the most elevation and rockiness, as the heightmap is mostly white in color. The next, *AM_Terre_HM_02* has some white around the edges with clouds of gray, resulting in a balanced level of elevation and rockiness. The final option, *FTUI_heightmap_*Test is nearly black with extremely light gray clouds brushing along the edges which will result in a predominately flat surface. Let us choose the second option, *AM_Terre_HM_02*, then select "Open" to load the heightmap into the Terrain Editor.

You will get a warning with the following text:

> *Image dimensions do not match dimensions of heightmap. Image size is 2048x2048, Heightmap size is 512x512. Would you like to clip the image, resize it, or cancel?*

Typically, you would want to resize your heightmap to fit using some external graphics application before importing the heightmap to your project. However, in our case, let us experiment with each of these options. The "Clip" option will remove any elevation values that exist outside the boundary of your project's current existing heightmap. The "Resize" option will either shrink or stretch elevation values to fit into your project's current existing heightmap. Resizing could make your terrain blocky-looking and unprofessional, but in this case, we are going to choose the "Resize" option and experiment with the result. Feel free to use the "Clip" option if you so choose.

As you can see, your viewport will now be filled with mountainous terrain that is likely extremely sharp and far too tall to be realistic. No worries, this is where a little bit of Lumberyard know-how will come in handy. As a default, Amazon Lumberyard sets the terrain's maximum height to 1024 meters. In fact, there are many heightmap properties that are set by default in Lumberyard. Lucky for us, these values are changeable, and they are very easy to change.

Changing Heightmap Properties

From the Terrain Editor window, in the menu bar select "Modify," and you will see all the heightmap properties available to change. The one we are particularly interested in for our example is the "Set Terrain Max Height" option. Click "Set Terrain Max Height," and a small dialog window will appear. We can now tell Lumberyard we would like our tallest mountain to be 225 meters tall, then click "OK" to lock in the value. In order to see this change reflected, however, you will need to reimport the heightmap from earlier. You should now see a very realistic looking terrain with just the right amount of rockiness.

While we are on the subject of heightmaps and heightmap properties, let's discuss a few of the other options from the "Modify" menu bar option in the Terrain Editor window. The first, "Make Isle," will sink the heightmap so that is surrounded by ocean. Keep in mind, however, that when this option is selected, its effects cannot be undone. I would advise that if you intend to experiment with this functionality that you save your level beforehand, so that you can test it out without having to worry about messing anything you have already created. The next option from the "Modify" menu bar option is the "Remove Ocean" option. Selecting this option does not actually remove the ocean; however, it simply sets the ocean's level to -100,000 meters, so it is completely out of view. Following the "Remove Ocean" option is the "Set Ocean Height" option, which allows you to set the height of the ocean in meters. After that, we have the "Set Terrain Max Height" option, which we have already used, but again it just sets the maximum height in meters for the tallest mountain on your terrain. Next, the "Set Unit Size" option will allow you to set the meters-per-texel size of the heightmap, which we covered in Chapter 3.

The next few options are options that will likely get used the most, as they offer capabilities to polish your terrain by making it look more realistic. The first of these, "Flatten," will flatten terrain either to a higher point or lower point within the viewport, depending on whether a positive or negative value is given. Following "Flatten" is "Smooth," which will attempt to move hard edges from a heightmap. Select this option when your mountains look unrealistically jagged or sharp. For the purposes of the example game, I will go ahead and select this option. As you can see, when this option is selected, your terrain softens out, making it look more and more realistic. This is an action that can be repeated multiple times. While "Smooth" will remove all of the hard edges from your heightmap, the next option "Smooth Slope" will only attempt to remove hard edges from steep areas, and the "Smooth Beaches/Coast" option will only attempt to remove hard edges from flatter areas of your heightmap.

The next option "Normalize" is interesting because it will guarantee that every shade of gray from white to black on the grayscale spectrum is used between zero and the height value you have specified for "Max Height." The next two options reduce the range of the heightmap mountains: the first "(Light)" will make all heightmap mountains slightly smaller, while the second "(Heavy)" will make the heightmap mountains a great deal smaller.

If at any point you decide that you would like a clean slate to wipe all the heightmap data you created, the next option is appropriately named "Erase Terrain," and it will do just that. This option will delete any and all heightmap data you have input into the Terrain Editor. The final two options are "Resize Terrain" and "Invert Terrain." "Invert Terrain" will take all white spots on your heightmap and turn them black and take all black spots on your heightmap and turn them white. Shades of gray will of course be flipped as well from light to dark and from dark to light. This will result in the same terrain you had, just inverted, in other words, rocky, mountainous terrain will result in a terrain with deep cave-like valleys. "Resize Terrain" allows you the option to change your heightmap resolution as well as your meters per texel in a separate window, shown in Figure 4-3.

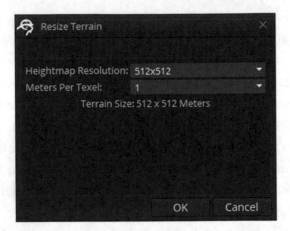

Figure 4-3. *In the heightmap properties, you can choose the option to resize your terrain's heightmap resolution. Keep in mind, however, that doing so will result in the undo-queue being cleared*

Painting Your Own Heightmap

We are going to tap into your creative side a bit in this section. While importing existing heightmaps is easy, it does not allow us the freedom of creating our own terrain that we can be proud of and say we did all on our own. If you have a heightmap imported already, erase it by using the "Erase Terrain" option within modify menu, discussed in the previous section to give us a fresh heightmap canvas to create on.

To paint your heightmap, open the Terrain Editor to the freshly clean heightmap view, and hover your mouse over the viewport behind the Terrain Editor. You will see either a single green circle (if your brush's inside radius is equal to your brush's outside radius) or two green circles if your radii are different. By clicking and dragging, you can modify your terrain this way, but the easiest way is to paint directly to the heightmap, as you have a larger canvas. Painting terrain directly to the viewport can result in blocky terrain that is isolated to one area of your game area, which is not optimal.

When hovering your mouse over the heightmap canvas, you will see a yellow circle, as shown in Figure 4-4. Clicking and dragging along the heightmap canvas will paint terrain which you can see as reflected by the change in grayscale color on the areas in which you have just painted terrain.

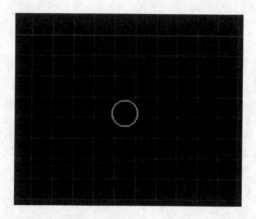

Figure 4-4. *The yellow circle indicates where on the heightmap grid you are about to make modifications to your terrain*

While developing, there will be times when you want to do different things with your brush to create different details. You may not always want to create mountain ranges, for example, you may want to flatten out some rocky object you've just created. The capability to change what type of brush you are currently using as well as the ability to change other aspects of your brush settings are available on the far-right side of the Terrain Editor window in a section called "Brush Settings," as shown in Figure 4-5.

Figure 4-5. *The Brush Settings section of the Terrain Editor window allows you to change various aspects of the current terrain brush you are using*

To begin, there are four main buttons at the top named "Flatten," "Smooth," "Rise/Lower," and "Pick Height." Selecting one of the first three of these options will load a different terrain brush, which will allow you to create different terrain features, while selecting the "Pick Height" button will allow you to change the height value of your brush based on the height of another space of terrain.

The "Flatten" brush will flatten terrain at a specified height and diameter when the brush is drawn on the heightmap editor. The specified height can be changed three ways:

- Type the height value in the "Height" input box below the brush buttons.

- Use the "Height" slider to change the height value.

- Use the "Pick Height" button, which will enable an eyedropper tool. When you click the area in the terrain whose height you would like to select, you will notice that both the "Height" input box as well as the "Height" slider values will update to reflect the height at the specified location in the terrain.

The "Rise/Lower" brush allows you to either decrease or increase terrain in the location the brush is clicked and dragged across, which is what you would use to create mountains or hills, for example. The last of the main terrain brushes, "Smooth," can be clicked and dragged across selected areas in the terrain where sharp gradients exist in order to smooth over those areas. This will allow you to smoothen out only targeted, selected areas, while the "Smooth" option in the heightmap properties settings will smoothen out your entire terrain. Both "Flatten" and "Rise/Lower" have several customizable buttons for you to utilize while building your terrain that utilize slider bar adjustment as well as input box.

"Outside Radius" will increase or decrease the outer most edge of your brush for larger or smaller additions to your terrain. This can be adjusted by either the slider bar by clicking and dragging to resize or using the input box. The input box allows you to either type your chosen size or use the increase or decrease arrows to change the size.

"Inside Radius" behaves similarly but is for the innermost radius of your brush. Think of this as the "peak" of your mountain. The smaller your inner radius the more of a peak you will create. Meanwhile the larger your inner radius the shape will resemble more of a column. Adjusting this size can be done using the slider or input box in the same way as previously stated for "Outside Radius." This is not adjustable for "Smooth" and "Pick Height" brushes.

Note   When increasing the radii of your brush, the size of the "Inner Radius" will never increase larger than your "Outside Radius." The largest your "Inner Radius" can be is equal to the "Outside Radius." The slider bar is built in such a way that when increasing the "Inner Radius" to the same size or larger than the "Outside Radius," the size of the "Outside Radius" will dynamically adjust as well.

Directly between the radius adjustment sections is a checkbox for "Sync all Radius for all Types." When selected, this option will hold your radius settings across the "Flatten," "Smooth," and "Rise/Lower" brush settings for uniformity and can be selected while in "Smooth" and "Pick Height" brushes.

"Hardness" adjusts how much of an impression your brush will make. When the hardness is lower, the terrain will be softer, but when the hardness is increased, the sharper the jump will be between outer and inner radii. Think of this as the difference between a rolling hill and a lone mountain. The "Hardness" of your brush in conjunction with the radii settings will form very different terrains.

"Height" is the setting that adjusts how high the terrain is raised or lowered depending on your other brush settings. This behaves differently regarding the size of your radii and hardness. "Smooth" does not allow customization of this option, while it is available to adjust for "Pick Height" and is the only adjustable button for that brush.

"Noise Settings" is an option to turn on for only the "Flatten" and "Rise/Lower" brushes. This will add random adjustments to the terrain for a more natural look.

"Reposition Objects" and "Reposition Vegetation" can be selected to adjust your objects or vegetation to realign with the newly modified terrain. This will keep both on top of your terrain. We will discuss adding objects in a later chapter and adding vegetation later in this chapter.

Once you are familiar with the brush settings, take the time to experiment with each of them, remembering that you can easily erase any changes you make completely by using the option "Erase Terrain" in the modify drop-down menu. Once you have a terrain that you have created all on your own, let us suppose you would like to take that terrain and export the heightmap for use in future levels. In the menu bar, select "File," then "Export Heightmap." Amazon Lumberyard will open a Windows File Explorer window that will allow you to save the location of your heightmap. Save it in the default directory that it opens to as "MyHeightmap.bt," and click "Save." To test that your new heightmap was exported properly, feel free to use the "Erase Terrain" method, followed by the "Import Heightmap" function outlined earlier in the chapter.

Otherwise, if you would rather want to let the Amazon Lumberyard Editor handle your terrain editing for you, this is entirely possible. In the menu bar, select the "Tools" option, and you will see in the drop-down list there will be an item for "Generate Terrain...." Select the "Generate Terrain" option from the drop-down list, and a terrain generator window will appear, as shown in Figure 4-6.

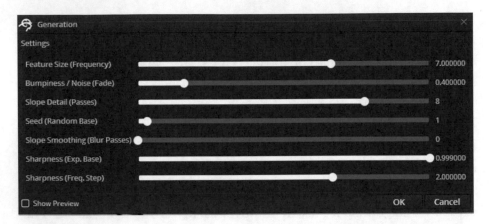

Figure 4-6. *The Terrain Generation tool is for those who want to generate a professional looking terrain at the click of a button*

You will notice that the terrain generator has many options to experiment with before generation. The first of these, "Feature Size (Frequency)," changes the number of peaks your generated terrain will have. For example, if you change this selection to the lowest option, your terrain generator will likely create a heightmap terrain with one mountain, whereas if you set this value to the highest option, it is likely your terrain will be extremely rocky.

The next option is "Bumpiness / Noise (Fade)," which in my opinion is best left at its default setting. This changes the amount of variation in height your terrain will have. Too little noise and your terrain will look very soft, smooth, and almost cartoon, while having too much noise will leave your terrain looking like a spiky ball.

Next is the "Slope Detail (Passes)" option, which will change the level of detail slopes of mountains and hills will have. If you are attempting to create a desert scene, you may opt to set this value slightly on the lower side, as you will not want a great deal of rockiness. Alternatively, if you are creating a rocky mountain with jagged cliffs and edges, you will want this setting to be high. Essentially, the number that corresponds with the slider will determine the number of times the slope detail effect is applied to the terrain to generate.

The next setting that can be changed in the terrain generator window is the "Seed (Random Base)" option, which will allow you to set the amount of random variation to be applied to the heightmap that will be generated. The higher the seed, the more variation the generated terrain will have.

The second-to-last option, "Slope Smoothing (Blur Passes)" does exactly what it sounds like. It will smoothen out slopes when the terrain is generated. The slider corresponds to the number of times that the smoothing effect is applied to the noise filter.

The last two options are similar, as both deal with the sharpness of the generated terrain. "Sharpness (Exp. Base)" sets the sharpness of the surface, while "Sharpness (Freq. Step)" allows you to set the number of times the sharpness filter is applied to the generated terrain.

Keep in mind that if you so choose to use the terrain generator instead of importing a heightmap or painting your own heightmap, you will still have the ability to export the terrain for use in future levels. It is also important to note that the Amazon Lumberyard Editor does not require you to erase the existing terrain before generating a new one, the generator will clear all heightmap data prior to generating new terrain.

Adding a Pop of Color

Now that we have nice mountainous terrain, we need to add some realistic color to it, like some grassy greens or sandy beiges. We can do this easily by using megatextures provided by Amazon Lumberyard or by painting them ourselves using texture layer painters. Let us get started by introducing what texture layers are, how to create them, and how to use them, then we will move on to using megatextures, in addition to how to import and export textures to be used across levels.

Texture Layers

Texture layers will be used when we want to create terrain coloration that does not already exist in some premade megatexture, which we will talk about later. The great thing about creating texture coloration in Amazon Lumberyard is that it provides you the ability to manipulate layers in order to establish rules like wanting a specific green color to be below a certain elevation; when you begin painting that color onto your terrain, if your brush touches any height about that elevation constraint, the texture will not be applied. Another reason using texture layers is preferred is that if you want to remove all areas of a certain color or texture rather than having to change your brush and find all of the areas with that texture or color, you can just remove that layer and immediately all instances will all vanish while leaving all color and texture you *do* want to be there remaining.

To get started, we first need to ensure that the textures provided by Amazon Lumberyard have been pulled into our game appropriately. While this should be handled when the StarterGame gem is added to the project, Amazon Lumberyard is still in beta, so it is always a good idea to double check things that should be handled by automation. In your file explorer, navigate to your project's textures directory, located at

```
C:\Amazon\Lumberyard\<Lumberyard_Version>\dev\MyFirstGame\
textures
```

If either this folder does not exist, this folder is empty, or this folder does not contain a folder titled "Natural" or "Terrain," you will need to follow the following steps. If this folder contains "Natural," "Terrain," and "Heightmaps" folders, feel free to skip ahead to the next section. To manually get the resources provided by Amazon Lumberyard into your project's texture directory, navigate to the StarterGame Textures directory, located at

```
C:\Amazon\Lumberyard\<Lumberyard_Version>\dev\StarterGame\Textures
```

80

Once in this location, use the keyboard key-combination Ctrl+A to select all items within this folder followed by the key-combination Ctrl+C simultaneously to copy all the selected items. Navigate back to your project's textures directory, and paste the items into the directory by using the keyboard combination Ctrl+V. Keep in mind, you will likely need to close the Amazon Lumberyard Editor throughout this process in order to allow these materials and assets to update appropriately within the editor for later use.

Terrain Texture Layers Editor

Before we begin painting textures onto our terrain, we need to set up layer definitions. While you can do this at any point in time, it is recommended to do it before you begin working on terrain coloration so that you do not have to keep flipping back and forth between different tools within the Lumberyard Editor. To begin, open the Terrain Texture Layers Editor by selecting the "Tools" selection in the Terrain Editor followed by selecting the "Terrain Texture Layers" option. Alternatively, if your Editors toolbar is visible, select the "Open Terrain Texture Layers Editor" option, shown in Figure 4-7.

Figure 4-7. *Opening the Terrain Texture Layers Editor through the Editors toolbar is likely the easiest method of opening the tool, assuming the Editors toolbar is displayed in your editor window*

When the Terrain Texture Layers Editor is open, as you can tell from Figure 4-8, there are many options to select from the left-side menu, and you will already have one default layer, which will be the gray color that currently covers your terrain.

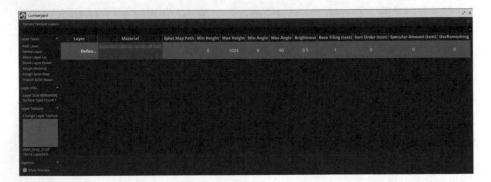

Figure 4-8. *The Terrain Texture Layers Editor is used for organizing texture layers, assigning materials to certain layers, and setting the layer indexes across your project*

To start, let us go over the options that are available within the Terrain Texture Layers Editor left-side menu. As you can likely tell, each task is associated with a group that helps organize the list of tasks. The first group list is the "Layer Tasks" group.

The first task, "Add Layer," creates a new terrain texture layer with default settings. To rename this newly created layer, double-click the name of the layer (by default this will be named "NewLayer") and assign it a new name. There are two settings that will need to be changed that will affect the look of your terrain layer: the texture and the material.

To change the material of a texture layer, click the link text in the "Material" column of the layer you would like to change the material of. This will open a window to the Material Editor, which was discussed in Chapter 2. Select the material you would like to use for your layer, then close the Material Editor window. You will notice that the material change will not yet be reflected in the Terrain Texture Layers Editor. To assign the material that was selected in the Material Editor to the selected layer, click the "Assign Material" option in the left-side menu of the Terrain Texture Layers Editor, and the material listed on the layer should now be updated.

To change the layer texture of a texture layer, select the layer, then in the left-side menu of the Terrain Texture Layers Editor, choose the option

"Change Layer Texture." This will open a window titled "Pick Texture," shown in Figure 4-9.

Figure 4-9. *The Pick Texture window allows you to preview the texture file before assigning it to a texture layer*

From this view, select the texture (.tif) file you would like to assign to the selected texture layer from the Natural/Terrain directory that we ensured existed in our project earlier in the chapter. Once you have selected the terrain texture file you would like to assign, click the orange "OK" button in the bottom right-hand corner of the window. You will notice that unlike assigning materials, the texture file will automatically be applied to the texture layer without any further effort to put forward.

The next option on the left-side menu of the Terrain Texture Layers Editor is the "Delete Layer" button, which is self-explanatory. Keep in mind when deleting texture layers that it is required to have at least one texture layer left over, so this button will do nothing if clicked when there is only one existing texture layer. Also keep in mind that this will not remove any painted areas that already exist on your game terrain.

The next two options work together to set the layer indexes in the list of texture layers, named "Move Layer Up" and "Move Layer Down." To use these, select a layer from the list, and click either the "Move Layer Up" option if you would like the layer to be higher in the list of texture layers or the "Move Layer Down" option to place the layer lower on the list.

The next left-side menu option is the "Assign Material" option which, as we have already discussed, will assign a selected material file to the selected texture layer.

The next two options allow you to use splat maps, which we will not be using for the purposes of this text; however, I will still walk through the process of assigning and importing them. Like the material assignment process, the use of splat maps requires a certain order of operations to be utilized. First, you need to assign splat maps to a texture layer by selecting the layer and clicking the "Assign Splat Map" option. This will open a Windows File Explorer window that you will use to navigate to the splat map bitmap file. Once the file is selected, click the "Open" button in the File Explorer. Similar to the material assignment process, you should not yet see any change being indicated until selecting the "Import Splat Maps" option from the left-side menu, which will rebuild the weight map for the terrain using the splat maps you have just assigned.

Note   A splat map is an 8-bit bitmap file that contains weight information for the terrain map vertices. These files are monochrome images similar to heightmaps, but unlike holding height data like a heightmap would, these hold weight data for a certain texture layer.

The next item in the left-side menu of the Terrain Texture Layers Editor is the "Layer Info" group which is not directly editable. This group just holds information about the layer size as well as the surface type count.

Following the Layer Info is the layer texture group, which we discussed how to change earlier in this section.

The final group in the menu is titled "Options," which only contains a checkbox titled "Show Preview," which is selected by default. When this checkbox is selected, you will see a preview of what the texture will look like on each layer from the list of all layers. When the checkbox is unselected, you will only see a list of layer names and information, without the texture previews available. The difference in having this option selected and unselected is demonstrated in Figure 4-10, where the left-side image shows the "Show Preview" option being selected and the right-side image shows the "Show Preview" option being unselected.

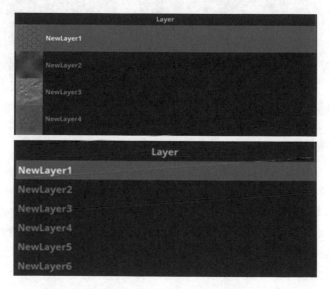

Figure 4-10. *Having the "Show Preview" option selected shows you what texture is assigned to a layer; however, it does limit the amount of layers you can see at a glance*

When creating your game, it is obvious that you would not want to redefine all the texture layer settings that you have used in one level to another level. It would be more efficient to combine all layer settings into a file, then, when a new level is created, import that file in order to reuse those layer settings. Amazon Lumberyard supports this texture layer export capability by clicking the icon that looks like two arrows pointing to the right, just below the "X" close button, shown in Figure 4-11. This will display a selection menu with the options "File," "Layer," and "Preview." Select the "File" option, and either press "E" on your keyboard or select the option "Export Layers...." A Windows File Explorer window will appear, allowing you to select the directory in which you would like to save your texture layer settings file, which will be denoted by the filename suffix "∗.lay".

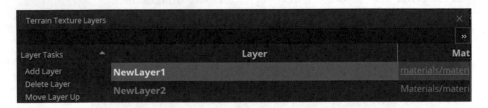

Figure 4-11. *The two arrows pointing to the right underneath the "X" close button in the Terrain Texture Layers Editor displays a menu list of useful tools*

Importing these layer texture files requires a similar process. Select the same menu icon from the Terrain Texture Layers Editor, once again select "the "File" option, this time however, instead of pressing "E" or selecting "Export Layers..." press "I" or select the option "Import Layers...." This will open a Windows File Explorer window that will allow you to select the "∗.lay" texture layer file to import. Once you have selected the file, select "Open," and the layers will be imported to the Layers Editor window. When texture layers are imported, the "Show Preview" button will be deselected, so if you would like to see previews for the newly imported texture layers, you will have to reselect the "Show Preview" option.

Close the texture editor once you've created some textures you want to use for the game. Once you do, if you click the "Terrain Texture" button from the viewport, you will now see your added layers.

Painting Texture Layers onto Your Terrain

Now that we have some texture layers defined, it is time to paint them onto our game's terrain to see what they look like in action. To do so, open the Terrain Tool by going to "Tools" in the menu bar of the Amazon Lumberyard Editor and selecting the "Terrain Tool" option. The Terrain Tool has seven options for terrain modification: "Modify," "Holes," "Vegetation," "Environment," "Layer Painter," "Move Area," and "Mini Map."

Selecting the "Modify" option will give you the same terrain modification tool that you would see in the Terrain Editor, discussed earlier in the chapter. The "Holes" option allows you to essentially erase an area of terrain by making or removing holes that exist within the terrain. "Vegetation" will give you the ability to add grass, trees, and other vegetation to your game, which we will talk about in depth further on in the chapter. "Environment" allows you to set a myriad of terrain settings, each with self-explanatory properties such as "Water Material," "Fog view distance," and "Moon Size," to name a few. There are many environment modifications you can add to your game, and with more practice, you will become familiar with them. The option in the Terrain Tools window that we are interested in for painting our texture layers onto our terrain is the "Layer Painter" option. Select "Layer Painter" now, and the window will change to display the layer painter tools, as shown in Figure 4-12.

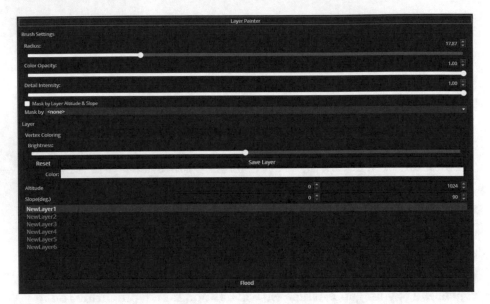

Figure 4-12. *The Layer Painter editor allows you to tweak brush settings and paint layers created in the Terrain Texture Layers Editor onto your game's terrain*

There are two groups of settings within the Layer Painter window: "Brush Settings" and "Layer" settings. Before we begin painting our layers onto our game terrain, let us look at what some of these options will change.

Brush Settings

The first option, "Radius," will set the radius of the paint brush used to paint the texture onto the terrain. The higher the radius, the more area on the terrain will be affected. Use a lower radius setting for painting more detailed areas of your terrain. You can change the radius by either typing the numeric value of the radius within the radius input box, using the slider associated with the radius input, or by using the keyboard shortcuts "[" to increase the brush size or "]" to decrease the brush size.

Each layer can have its own color. For example, if you have three layers of grass with the same texture, you can set each of these layers to have a different shade of green which will make your terrain look more realistic. The next option in the brush settings group is "Color Opacity," which lets you specify how much color will come through when applying the layer to your terrain. If you think of the brush as a paint brush in real life, the "Color" opacity setting essentially would describe how hard the brush is pressed down onto the canvas. The higher the color opacity (or the harder the brush is pressed down), the more color will come through onto the terrain, while a lower setting will result in a fainter coloration. Similarly, the next option in the brush settings group "Detail Intensity" allows you to specify how detailed you would like your painted texture to be when applying the layer to the terrain. For both the color intensity and the detail intensity, you can use the slider associated with each to set their values, or you can use keyboard shortcuts.

To increase or decrease detail intensity via keyboard shortcuts, use Ctrl+] to increase the detail intensity or Ctrl+[to decrease the detail intensity. To increase or decrease color opacity via keyboard shortcuts, use Shift+] to increase the color opacity or Shift+[to decrease the color opacity. It is likely that there will be times in which you would like to increase or decrease both = settings simultaneously. To do this, use the keyboard command combination Shift+Ctrl+[to decrease both the detail intensity and color opacity settings or Shift+Ctrl+] to increase both the detail intensity and color opacity settings.

The next option in the brush settings will be the "Mask by Layer Altitude and Slope" checkbox. This setting works in tandem with the Altitude and Slope values which can be set in the layer settings for a specific layer. This option will set the material to only be painted between the layer's Altitude and Slope settings, which we will talk about more when we talk about layer settings. The "Mask by" option in the brush settings group tells the "Mask by Layer Altitude and Slope" which layer's Altitude and Slope values to consider when painting terrain.

Layer Settings

The first of the layer settings "Brightness" allows you to modify how bright the coloration of the material will be when painted onto the terrain. When this is changed, you need to click the "Save Layer" button to apply the changes. This can be reset at any point by selecting the "Reset" button. To change the color of a layer, click the color box in order to open the color selector which will modify the base color of the selected layer.

The next setting in the Layer Settings section is "Altitude," which allows you to set the altitude range at which you would like to mask the terrain for painting. For example, if your minimum altitude is 20 and your maximum altitude is 40 and you attempt to paint this texture layer onto an area in the terrain whose altitude is 20 or below or 40 or above, the brush will not be applied, as these altitudes are outside the specified boundaries. These "Altitude" and "Slope" settings are the values the brush setting "Mask by Layer Altitude and Slope" uses. Keep in mind each layer will have its own altitude and slope values.

Similar to the "Altitude" setting, the "Slope" setting allows you to set the slope range at which you would like to mask the terrain for painting. The numeric value in this slope setting will reflect the number of degrees in the slope. Brush strokes will only be applied to slopes within the specified range.

To change settings for different layers, select the layer from the layer list directly below the Altitude and Slope setting areas. Double-clicking a layer will open the Terrain Texture Layers Editor with the clicked layer selected within the editor.

If there is one main layer you would like to have across your entire terrain, the final option in the Layer Painter options "Flood" will allow you to do so. By clicking the button labeled "Flood," the selected layer will be applied across the entire game terrain.

Using Megatextures

Megatextures, or megaterrain textures, are a great way to cover the entire terrain all at once – if you have one available. Lucky for us, Amazon Lumberyard comes packaged with a megaterrain texture we can use. While textures from a megaterrain texture will be visible from any distance in the game, the quality of the terrain will be low until the camera moves closer to the terrain, at which point the megaterrain texture is replaced by terrain textures with a higher level of detail.

To import a megaterrain texture, open the Terrain Editor using the steps discussed earlier in the chapter, then click "Tools" in the menu bar, followed by the "Export/Import Megaterrain Texture" option, to display the window shown in Figure 4-13. Depending on what version of Amazon Lumberyard you have, you may not see this option. If this is the case, click "Game" in the menu bar, followed by "Terrain."

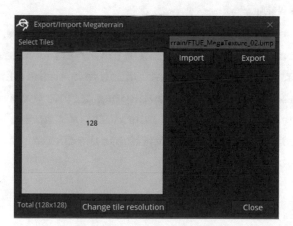

Figure 4-13. *The user interface for importing and exporting megaterrain textures in Amazon Lumberyard*

At the left, you will see a square titled "Select Tiles," with only one tile available. That is the result of our choosing to set meters per texel to 1 in Chapter 3 when we created the level. If your meters per texel setting was higher than 1, you would have multiple tiles to select here – each of which can have their own megaterrain texture.

At the bottom-left corner of the window is a "Change tile resolution" button that will allow you to change the resolution of the terrain tile in this window. Before this button will be active, you must select a tile sector so the engine knows which section of the terrain you would like to modify. To continue with importing the megatexture, select the single tile from the "Select Tiles" section, then click the "Import" button on the "Export/ Import Megaterrain" window, and a Windows File Explorer window will appear. Find the file called FTUE_MegaTexture_02 located at

```
Amazon\Lumberyard\<Lumberyard_Version>\dev\MyFirstGame\
textures\Terrain
```

Select this file, and click "Open." You will see that your terrain in the viewport will be entirely enveloped with this megatexture that you have selected. Click "Close" when you are done.

Exporting megaterrain textures follows a similar process. Open the Terrain Editor, click the "Tools" button in the menu bar, followed by the "Export/Import Megaterrain Texture" option to open the window shown in Figure 4-13. Select the tile that has the megatexture you would like to export on it, then click the "Export" button. This will open a Windows File Explorer window so that you can choose the directory in which the megatexture is saved.

Vegetation

We now have realistic looking terrain and a coloration that makes it look professional, but we are still missing one thing that will make our terrain stand out above others – vegetation. We need rocks, trees, and grass if we want our terrain look like a real place.

Before we begin, we need to make sure we have the vegetation objects provided by Amazon Lumberyard within our "MyFirstGame" directory. Similar to the situation we discussed earlier in the chapter about terrain heightmaps and megatextures, this process should be handled by the Project Configurator, but as Amazon Lumberyard is in beta, it is possible and common for this step to be skipped. Navigate to your "MyFirstGame" directory to see if a folder called "Objects" exists. If the folder either does not exist, or the folder exists but is empty, navigate to the StarterGame dev directory located here:

`Amazon\Lumberyard\<Lumberyard_Version>\dev\StarterGame`

Select the "Objects" folder, press the keyboard combination Ctrl+C to copy the folder, then navigate back to your "MyFirstGame" directory located at

`Amazon\Lumberyard\<Lumberyard_Version>\dev\MyFirstGame\`

Paste the copied folder into your "MyFirstGame" directory by using the keyboard combination Ctrl+V. Keep in mind you may want to restart your Amazon Lumberyard Editor if it is currently running and does not reflect any changes.

To begin adding vegetation to your terrain, first open the vegetation editor by going to the menu bar and selecting "Tools," followed by "Terrain Tool." From the button group on the Terrain Tool, select "Vegetation" to open a window, as shown in Figure 4-14. Depending on what version of Amazon Lumberyard you have, you may not see this option. If this is the case, click "Game" in the menu bar, followed by "Terrain," followed once more by "Edit Vegetation."

Figure 4-14. *The vegetation editor allows you to add professional level vegetation to your terrain. On the left, settings for which vegetation you will be painting onto the terrain. On the right, the option to remove duplicated vegetation and preview which vegetation will be painted.*

As you will see, there are several buttons at the top of the vegetation editor. The first, most important button is the "Add Vegetation Object" button. Selecting this will bring up a window that allows you to select which vegetation object (found in the Objects folder we ensured existed in our directory) you would like to add to your terrain. Select the object and click the orange "OK" button in the bottom right-hand corner of the screen. For reference, most vegetation objects will be in the Objects directory:

`MyFirstGame\Objects\Natural\Vegetation`

The Objects\Natural directory will also have caves, rocks, and other items you can use to spruce up your terrain, but for now we will focus solely on vegetation. I will add the object `am_cedar_group.cgf`.

You will see that your list of objects in the vegetation editor will now be updated to have the object you have selected be listed. You may notice that it will be under a drop-down called "Default." This is called a vegetation category, and it is one way Amazon Lumberyard helps you create more natural looking terrain by allowing you to paint multiple types of vegetation onto your terrain at once, blending the objects naturally. By selecting the entire category, all objects that exist within that category will be modified or painted at the same time, while selecting a single object within that category will only modify or paint the object selected.

Selecting a vegetation object or category will bring up a myriad of settings that can be changed on that object or category, as shown in Figure 4-15.

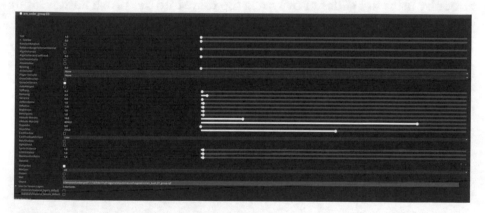

Figure 4-15. *Selecting a vegetation object will enable you to make many changes to that object*

There are several settings for vegetation, but we will start off with the basics. The first, "Size," changes the height of the object you will paint. When creating your terrain vegetation, you should keep in mind that in real life, trees are almost never all exactly the same height, so you should use the second setting "+ - SizeVar", which lets you set a value for height variation. This will enhance your vegetation details. For example, if you use "15" for size and "5" for SizeVar, all trees you paint will be between 10 and 20 height, as the size variation is set to the size + or - the size variation value.

The next thing to consider when painting terrain vegetation is that if all of your trees are aligned with their bases at the same angle, your terrain will not look natural. Check the "RandomRotation" box on the object's settings in order to tell Amazon Lumberyard to rotate each vegetation object to a different degree. This, paired with the size variation, will allow you to create more natural looking terrain.

When you are ready to begin painting your vegetation objects onto your terrain, change the Brush Radius setting in the vegetation editor either by using the slider or by typing the value into the Brush Radius input box, then click the gray "Paint Objects" button. Click and drag along your viewport, and watch your terrain come to life. Be mindful, however, to only paint vegetation in areas that your game character will be encountering. For example, if your character will be walking down a road, maybe only heavily vegetate the sides of the road in which your character will be traveling. Creating too many vegetation objects will take an immense amount of processing power and may make your game slower.

Of the many buttons at the top of the vegetation editor, the next is "Clone Vegetation Object." To use this, select a vegetation object from your list, and click the "Clone Vegetation Object" button to make an exact copy of the selected vegetation object.

The next button is "Replace Vegetation Object." If you paint your terrain with a certain type of flowers, for example, the `am_grass_flower_white_group.cgf` vegetation object, and decide that your terrain would actually be better off with purple flowers, this button will allow you to replace all instances of white flowers with purple flowers without having to erase your vegetation and start over. To do so, select the vegetation object you would like to replace, the "Replace Vegetation Object" button, and select a new vegetation object to replace it with – for our example, this would be the `am_grass_flower_purple_group.cgf` object, then click the orange "OK" button at the bottom of the window.

When you added your first vegetation object, Amazon Lumberyard automatically created a "Default" category for you. The next button "Add Vegetation Category" allows you to manually create categories so that you can organize your vegetation objects a bit nicer. For example, you could create a vegetation category called "Grasses" and another vegetation category called "Trees," and so on, in order to have all of your grasses or trees in their own category. This will make creating vegetative terrains much simpler, as you will be able to easily identify the location of all of your vegetation objects.

The next option, "Remove Vegetation Object," does exactly what it says. When a vegetation object or category is selected and the "Remove Vegetation Object" button is selected, the object or category will be removed from the list, and all of the instances in which that object or category exists on the terrain will also be cleared.

"Export Vegetation" is the next option, and it will be useful for you if you have made many tweaks and changes to the vegetation objects in your list or if you have set up your categories in a way that you would like to reuse. Similarly, the next button, "Import Vegetation," allows you to take previously exported vegetation and import it to your current level for reuse.

Use the next option sparingly, as it is "Distribute Vegetation on Whole Terrain." Whatever vegetation object or vegetation category you have currently selected will be placed randomly across the entire terrain when this button is selected, which as we discussed earlier, depending on the vegetation object could cause serious performance issues. This should only be used for something like grass or rocks.

The next option is "Clear Terrain," and it should be used when you want to clear all instances of the selected vegetation object or category from the terrain, but you would still like to have the vegetation object or category in the list of available objects.

"Scale Vegetation" is the next button in the group. With a vegetation object or category selected, click the "Scale Vegetation" button to increase the height of previously existing terrain objects. While you can change the size and size variation of vegetation objects to be painted, this is how you will change the size of terrain objects that have already been painted.

With two vegetation objects selected, the next button allows you to merge the two objects into one vegetation object. It is the "Merge Vegetation" button.

Last but not least, "Put Selection into Category" is the final option. When an object is selected that does not already exist within a category, selecting this button will provide you the ability to assign the object to a category. Alternatively, you are able to drag the object into the desired category as well.

Take some time to experiment with the vegetation of your game – it is what will set your project apart from others. There are many vegetation objects that Amazon Lumberyard provides – so you should be able to create gorgeous terrain in no time.

Time of Day

In the world you create, you may want to change how long your days are. For example, you may want to only have 2 in-game hours be daylight in order for your character to collect resources to survive the 22-hour eerie night. There are two primary tools to change daytime settings – the Time of Day Editor and the Sun Trajectory tool. Because the Time of Day Editor is such a complex tool, we will start off focusing on the Sun Trajectory tool, then we will discuss a few aspects of the Time of Day Editor.

To open the editor for modifying Sun Trajectory settings, first open the Terrain Editor following the steps detailed earlier in the chapter. Next, in the menu bar choose the "Tools" option, followed by "Sun Trajectory tool..." in the drop-down list, which will open a window that looks like Figure 4-16.

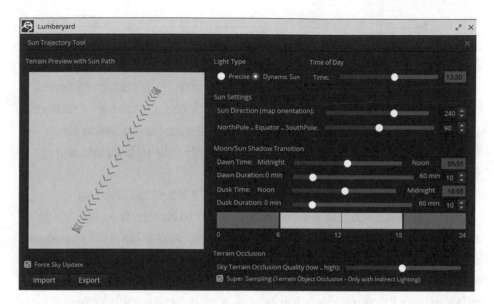

Figure 4-16. *The Sun Trajectory tool is a simple user interface that allows you to edit how long your days will be, and how your sun will travel through your game*

On the left, there is a window full of red arrows in a line. This line is the trajectory that your game's sun will follow. The red arrows point in the direction in which your sun will travel along this path. If you have already created Sun Trajectory settings, you can use the "Import" button in the bottom left-hand corner of the window to pull those settings in quickly. Similarly, once you have made changes to your current Sun Trajectory settings, clicking the "Export" button in the bottom left-hand corner of the screen will allow you to export settings for use in future levels.

One of the main Sun Trajectory tool settings controls you will want to recognize is the "Time of Day." Changing the time of day here will set the time that the game will start at. Keep in mind that all times within both the Sun Trajectory tool as well as the Time of Day Editor are in 24-hour time. You can change the time of day either by using the slider or typing a 24-hour formatted time within the "Time of Day" input box.

The next two settings that we will likely want to change will be the "Sun Direction" and "NorthPole .. Equator .. SouthPole" settings. By moving the slider for "Sun Direction," you will be able to see in real time the sun's trajectory change in the left-hand side of the Sun Trajectory editor. Similarly, when you move the slider for "NorthPole .. Equator .. SouthPole," you will see the trajectory change as well. Changing these two settings together will change the tilt of your "planet," affecting where and how your sun will travel around it.

The final settings we will change are the "Moon/Sun Shadow Transition" settings. This is what will allow us to change how long days and nights are. The first setting is "Dawn Time," and this allows you to set a specific time in which dawn will begin. Using the input box allows you to input a specific time, while using the slider allows you to experiment with this setting a bit more, changing how many hours past midnight (00:00) you would like dawn to begin. The next setting is "Dawn Duration," which will be in minutes. This setting will allow you to set how long you would like the transition between dawn and daytime to be. Again, you can either use the input box to specify the number of minutes dawn should last, or you can use the slider to experiment. The last two of the Moon/Sun Shadow Transition settings will do the same thing as the first two; however, instead of modifying the dawn times and transitions, you will be modifying the dusk times and transitions.

All of these "Moon/Sun Shadow Transition" settings will update the daytime graph that you will see at the bottom of the Sun Trajectory tool. The yellow area in this graph will indicate the daytime time span, the purple/blue area will indicate the nighttime time span, and the black areas will indicate either the dawn or dusk transitions between nighttime and daytime. Close out the Sun Trajectory tool.

The last editor we will use to modify our game's terrain is the Time of Day Editor which, as previously stated, is a fairly complex editor, so we will only discuss how to change a few of the more important settings; it is still highly encouraged that you experiment on your own for many of the other settings.

From the Lumberyard Editor menu bar, open the Time of Day Editor by selecting "Tools," followed by "Other," and lastly selecting the "Time of Day" option. Alternatively, if your Editors toolbar is enabled, you can click the "Time of Day" Editor button, as shown in Figure 4-17.

Figure 4-17. *The Editors toolbar is the simplest way to open the Time of Day Editor*

Once the Time of Day Editor is open, you will see a window that has many settings to change and looks like Figure 4-18.

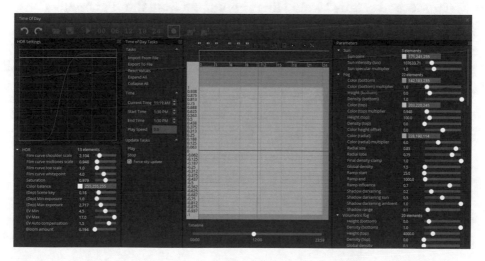

Figure 4-18. *The Time of Day Editor allows you to make many advanced changes to your game's daytime and nighttime settings*

While this editor has many options, it is rather intuitive since it is mostly full of sliders that are all relatively self-explanatory. There are two that I would like to point out that you do not necessarily need; however, they will add a nice professional touch to your game.

The first is the "Sun color" setting, which is the first option to change in the "Parameters" group on the right-hand side of the screen. Why would you want to change the color of the sun? Well, if your game is an icy-kingdom, you may want the light from the sun to emit a light-blue color to give your environment more of a colder look. Alternatively, if your game is on a beach or another warm oasis, you could change your color to more of a red-orange hue that will make the environment look warmer. To change this setting, click on the colored square next to "Sun color" which will bring up a color picker. Once your color has been selected, click the "OK" button in the bottom right-hand corner of the screen.

The second setting I would like to point out from the "Parameters" group are the "Fog" settings. If you are working on a game that perhaps has a haunted graveyard or swamp, consider changing the color of your fog to a greenish color by clicking the colored square next to "Color" under the fog category to open a color picker. Once your color has been selected, click the "OK" button in the bottom right-hand corner of the screen. This is also where you can change the fog density and height.

Now that you have a gorgeous terrain created full of color, vegetation, water, and mountains, I think it is finally time to talk about adding a character so you can get in and explore the world you have been creating. In the next chapter, we will add a character player, props, and buildings and discuss everything you will need to know about entities and slices.

CHAPTER 5

Entities and Slices

We now have professional terrain that is ready to be explored. Before we can explore this terrain, however, we need to create a character that we can control. To do that, we need to understand what entities, child entities, and slices are. More importantly, we need to know how to add these to our game and package them in such a way they can be reused in future levels. By the end of this chapter, you will have props lining your game terrain as well as a character that you can control in order to interact with your game objects. Amazon Lumberyard's starter game project comes packaged with assets that we can use to learn the engine – such as a boxes, robots, rocks, doors, walls, and more - including the character that we will use.

Verifying the Project Structure

Before we begin, like the terrain heightmaps and megatextures, we need to make sure the starter game objects were pulled into our "MyFirstGame" directory properly when we added the StarterGame gem in the Project Configurator. As I stated in Chapter 4, the Project Configurator should have handled this step; however, as Amazon Lumberyard is in beta, it is not uncommon for the configurator to skip a few steps, so we need to go manually verify that this was handled.

First, open your project directory, located in

```
C:\Amazon\Lumberyard\<Lumberyard_Version>\dev\MyFirstGame
```

© Jaken Chandler Herman 2019
J. C. Herman, *Beginning Game Development with Amazon Lumberyard*,
https://doi.org/10.1007/978-1-4842-5073-0_5

There are two folders in this directory we need to look for. The first folder is named "Objects." Verify that this folder exists and is not empty. The second folder is named "slices." Verify that this folder also exists and is also not empty. If both or either of these folders either do not exist or are empty, navigate to the StarterGame directory, located in

```
C:\Amazon\Lumberyard\<Lumberyard_Version>\dev\StarterGame
```

Click the "Objects" folder, then while holding the Ctrl button on your keyboard, select the "slices" folder. Navigate back to your project directory and either right-click the empty space within the directory and choose "Paste" or use the keyboard key-command Ctrl+V to paste these folders into your project directory. Keep in mind that if both folders existed but were empty, or if one folder existed but was empty, you will get a warning that a folder with the given name already exists. Select the "Replace" option to replace the existing folder with the copied "Objects" and "slices" folders within your project directory. If you already have the Amazon Lumberyard Editor open, I would recommend restarting it at this point.

Entities and the Entity Outliner

Any game element that will appear in the Entity Outliner, which we will discuss further in the chapter, is classified as an "Entity" or a "Slice." Entities are just game objects that we can move around and interact with. For example, props like boxes, buildings, camera objects, and even player objects are all considered entities.

If your Amazon Lumberyard is not currently open, open it now using the steps outlined in Chapter 2. To begin working with entities, objects, and slices, we need to discuss the area of the editor that these will be displayed in – the Entity Outliner.

By default, the Entity Outliner is open and is docked to the left side of the screen. If your Entity Outliner is not open and docked by default, or if you have accidentally closed it and are unsure of how to reopen it, navigate to the "Tools" option of the menu bar, and select "Entity Outliner" to open the Entity Outliner, shown in Figure 5-1.

Figure 5-1. *The Entity Outliner will show all entities and slices that exist on your game. This is the easiest place to handle the management of your entities.*

As you will notice, because of the template choice we made when creating our project, our Entity Outliner window already has an entity, "DefaultLevelSetup." Each entity within your project will have its own row in the Entity Outliner, and each of these entities will have a few options and indicators associated with them.

The first item you will see to the far left of the entity row will be an icon that indicates what type the entity is (i.e., an object or a slice). The following table contains different icon indicators as well as what they describe.

Icon	Description
White cube	A white cube indicates entities that are stand-alone entities, i.e., they are not part of a slice or a child to another entity.
Blue cube	Entities that are indicated by a blue cube are entities that *are* part of a slice instance.
Orange cube	Entities that are indicated by an orange cube have different component property values than the source slice; in other words, these entities have "overrides."
Lines	Entities that have lines associated with them, whether that line be coming from, or going to, the entity indicates a parent-child hierarchy between the entities.
Dot in bottom-right corner of cube	When an entity icon contains a dot in the bottom right-hand corner of the icon cube, this indicates that this is a parent entity that contains a child entity with an override.
Dark row shading	Shaded rows indicate an entity that is a slice root, which will be discussed later in the chapter.

The next items you will see on the entity row will be the entity name, followed by an eye icon as well as a lock icon to the right of the name. Selecting the eye icon will hide the entity from the viewport of your project but will not remove the entity from the game. This functionality is handy when you have multiple entities that look similar, because you can toggle the view on and off to discover which entity you have selected in the list. When the entity is not already visible in the viewport because it has previously been hidden, the icon will be an eye with a diagonal line through it. Selecting this icon will make the entity reappear within the viewport.

The lock icon to the far right of the entity row will prevent the entity from being modified in any way. This is useful when you have worked hard to get an entity just the way you would like it and want to prevent accidental slips of the mouse or deletions. Once an entity is locked, nothing can be changed on it except for its locked status – meaning you can always unlock the entity when you are ready to make changes again.

These icons in the entity row are not the only changes you can make to entities from the Entity Outliner, however. Right-clicking an entity gives you a wide array of options, as shown in Figure 5-2.

Figure 5-2. *Each entity within the Entity Outliner will have certain options associated with it. To access these options, right-click the entity from the Entity Outliner window.*

The first option on this list, "Create entity," actually has nothing to do with the selected entity at all. This option will show up even if you do not right-click an entity row but instead right-click anywhere within the Entity Outliner window. When selected, Amazon Lumberyard will create a new empty entity and place it into the Entity Outliner. It will be a 1x1x1 default entity with no material or actions associated with it. Using this option is not the only way to create an entity in Amazon Lumberyard, however.

It is also possible to add an entity from the Asset Browser window, which was discussed in length in Chapter 2.

To add an entity or slice to your game from the Asset Browser window, navigate to the entity you would like to add in the Asset Browser list, then click and drag the object into the Entity Outliner window, and the entity will be placed in your game. Alternatively, you can click and drag the object directly into the viewport to add entities or slices to your game.

The next option on this list is "Create child entity." This option allows you to tie two entities together. Any time the parent entity is moved, modified, or deleted, the child object will also be moved, modified, or deleted. Keep in mind, however, that because child entities are not parent entities, they can move freely without affecting the parent entity's position or status.

We will discuss the next two options "Create Slice..." and "Instantiate Slice..." later in the chapter when we talk about slices. The next option, duplicate, does exactly what it says. When this option is selected, the entity will be duplicated onto the viewport and within the Entity Outliner window. This does not link the entity to the newly duplicated in any way, so think of this as a copy-paste entity.

Next is "Delete," and there are actually two ways of handling this. You can either use this option to right-click the entity and select "Delete" to remove entities from the viewport and Entity Outliner, or you can select the entity and press the "Delete" button on your keyboard. If the deleted entity is a parent entity, the child objects associated with it will also be deleted when this option is selected.

After "Delete" is "Open Pinned Inspector," which we will discuss later in the chapter. This option is followed by "Rename," which like "Delete" can be handled in multiple ways. The first way to rename an entity would be to right-click the entity within the Entity Outliner and select this "Rename" option. The second is to double-click the entity name within the Entity Outliner window in slow succession. The third way to rename an entity or slice is through the inspector which, again, we will discuss later in the chapter.

The final option in the entity selection window is "Find in Viewport." This is another helpful way to see which entity you are modifying when you have multiple entities in your game. As your game grows, your Entity Outliner will fill up with a large number of entities. Selecting this option will highlight the entity within the viewport window, so you know exactly which entity you are modifying.

If we look above the list of entities within the Entity Outliner window, we see three tools we can use to filter our list of entities a little bit better. The first, most obvious tool is the search bar, at the far top left of the Entity Outliner window. If you know the name of the entity you would like to modify, you can search the name here to narrow down your list.

The next option, the one whose icon is a filter, allows you to filter entities by components that they contain. Components can be added and removed from within the inspector.

The next, and final, far-right option at the top of the Entity Outliner window contains the sort options for the Entity Outliner list, shown in Figure 5-3.

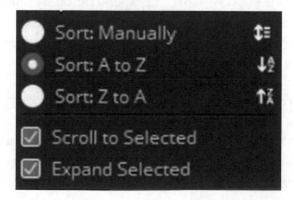

Figure 5-3. *The Entity Outliner sort menu allows you to change the order in which entities are listed, helping you find the entity you need faster*

The first option, "Sort: Manually", will be used when you want to rearrange the order of entities yourself. When this option is enabled, if entity X is listed below entity Y, but you would prefer that it be listed *above* entity Y, right-click entity X and select the option "Move Up." Similarly, if entity X is listed above entity Y, but you would like it to be listed *below* entity Y, right-click entity X and select the "Move Down" option.

The next two options will sort entities alphabetically either in order from A to Z or from Z to A, depending on which of the two options is selected. It should be noted that an entity who is a child of another entity will be sorted alphabetically by its *parent* entity. We will discuss child and parent entities in the next section of this chapter.

The next two options from the Entity Outliner sort menu are checkboxes that will help you find elements in the Entity Outliner from your viewport. If "Scroll to Selected" is marked as active, selecting an entity from within the viewport window will scroll either up or down, depending on where the entity is listed in the Entity Outliner so that it is accessible for editing quickly from the Entity Outliner list.

"Expand Selected" is useful when you have a great deal of child entities in your game. When this option is marked as active, selecting an entity from within the viewport window will expand the entity's parent entity, displaying the list of child entities it contains, if any. If the entity is not part of a child-parent contract, this function serves no real purpose.

Child and Parent Entities

We have mentioned child entities and parent entities quite a bit this chapter, but we still have not discussed what they are or why we would use them. A child entity is an entity that is created or modified to be linked to another existing entity, whereas a parent entity is an entity that has other entities linked to it. While this sounds a bit confusing at first, it will actually make more sense when you play around with this functionality. Any time an entity is marked as the child of another entity, any scaling or other transformative changes that are made to the parent entity are also reflected to all of its child entities.

For example, if you were to create a hollow box out of four rectangle entities, you could link three of the box's edges to one parent edge. Any time you would move the parent edge, all child edges would follow along. Any time you were to make the parent edge larger, all child edges would scale to match. This will keep you from having to make multiple changes to many different entities when working with a group that should all have relative uniformity. Keep in mind, however, that making transformative changes to a child entity will *not* be reflected to the parent.

A child entity can also be a parent entity, as well. Think of this hierarchy of parent-child entities by using the real-world example of grandparents. A parent can have a child, and that child can have a child, and so on. Changes made to any parent entity that contains child entities will be reflected to those child entities, but that change will never travel upward to the grandparents unless that change is directly made to the grandparent entities.

There are multiple different ways to create a child entity. The first, most obvious option would be to right-click the entity which you would like to be the parent entity, and select the option "Create child entity...." A child entity will be created, and you can add components to it, rename it, and modify it according to your preference.

Another method of creating a child entity would be to click and drag an asset from the Asset Browser window and drop the entity onto an existing entity, which you would like to be the parent entity. If you have already created the entity and would like to change it from being independent to be a child entity, click and drag the entity name from the Entity Outliner list and drop it onto the entity name which you would like to be the parent entity. The final way to create a child entity is through the entity Pinned Inspector, which we will discuss in the next section.

The Pinned Inspector

Earlier in the chapter, we briefly mentioned the entity Pinned Inspector, which was an option from the drop-down list we were shown when right-clicking an entity name from the entity list in the Entity Outliner window. Pick an entity from your list, or if one does not exist yet, create one and open the Pinned Inspector window, shown in Figure 5-4.

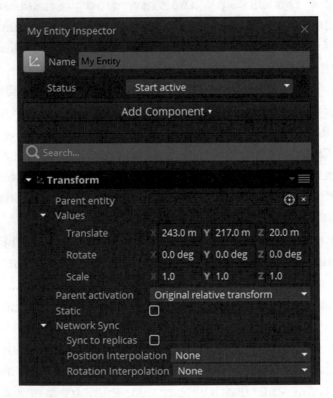

Figure 5-4. *An entity's Pinned Inspector window shows you all active components on an entity and allows you to modify them*

Directly beneath the title bar of the inspector that contains the entity's name is a green icon. This icon allows you to modify which icon you would like to represent the entity. Selecting this icon will drop down a select list with two options: "Set Default Icon" and "Set Custom Icon." By default, the icon will already be the default icon, so clicking this option without first selecting a new icon to represent the entity will do nothing. If, however, the icon had been previously changed to a custom icon, selecting this option will revert the icon to the default entity icon. Selecting the "Set Custom Icon" option will open a new window that allows you to pick a custom entity icon, if you have any custom icons created for your project.

The next element on the Pinned Inspector is the "Name" field, which allows you to rename your entity from this window rather than doing it via right-clicking the entity and choosing the "Rename" option.

After the "Name" field is the "Status" field, which allows you to change the status of the selected entity via the drop-down list shown in Figure 5-5.

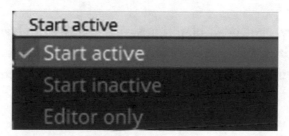

Figure 5-5. *The "Status" field within the entity Pinned Inspector window allows you to change the status of entities*

This will allow you to set entities as only being active when gameplay mode is not currently enabled, that is, you can set entities to "editor only" mode. By default, entities will start as active within a level. Selecting the drop-down menu for changing the status of entities will reveal the following options:

Option	Description
Start active	Entity will be active when the level starts. This is the default option.
Start inactive	Entity will be inactive when the level starts.
Editor only	The entity will only be active in editing mode. When gameplay mode begins, the entity will be marked as inactive.

After the "Status" field is the "Add Component" button. We will discuss components further in Chapter 6, but let us briefly explore the functionality of this button. Clicking the "Add Component" button will serve a drop-down list of all of your component options. To add a component, just choose the component from the list, and it will be added to your entity's component list.

The next area of the inspector is a list of components that exist on the entity, with a variety of options that can be changed on each of these components. The first item within this area is a search bar, which will search through the list of components on an entity by component name. Components names who do not match the search query will temporarily be hidden.

Every entity, even basic blank entities, will contain at least one component – the transform component. We will discuss the transform component in more detail in Chapter 6 when we discuss components in depth.

Slices

Throughout the course of not only this chapter but previous chapters as well, I have mentioned slices without going into much detail about what they are, or how they can be used to reuse entity groups easily.

A slice is merely an assortment of entities that is stored as a single asset object that can be reused across multiple levels within a project, or even across multiple different projects. For this to make more sense, let us create a slice before discussing them any further.

To create a slice, select one or more entities (if more than one, press Ctrl and select multiple) in the Entity Outliner, then right-click one of the selected entities, and choose the option "Create slice...." A "Save As..." Windows Explorer window will appear, allowing you to give your slice a name. Name this slice "My First Slice" and click the "Save" button.

Slices are saved as .slice files within your game project directory by default; however, when creating slices, you can choose to save them to another location although it is not recommended.

If only one entity was selected to create the slice or if the entities selected to create the slice existed with a parent-child relationship, the slice should have been created with no issue. You will get an error message saying that the slice could not be created, shown in Figure 5-6, if you attempt to create a slice from two or more entities that have no parent-child relationship.

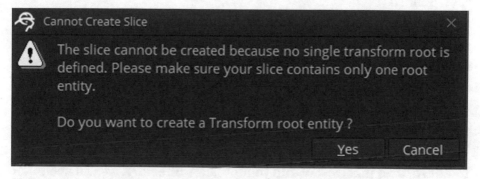

Figure 5-6. *The "Cannot Create Slice" message will appear when no single transform root is defined. Single transform root entities can be created from this message by clicking the "Yes" button.*

The reason this will appear is because if the two entities do not have any relationship to one another and you attempt to create a slice containing the two of them, Amazon Lumberyard does not know which entity's transform component you would like to use by default. As we stated earlier in the chapter, every entity will have a transform component. While this is true, a child entity will inherit the transform component properties of its parent, meaning there is one transform "root." This is why when the parent entity is moved along the x-, y-, or z-axis, the child entity is moved as well.

You can either have Amazon Lumberyard create a transform root entity by clicking the "Yes" button in the bottom right-hand corner of the "Cannot Create Slice" message window, or, if you would like to define the transform root yourself, click the "Cancel" button.

To define the transform root yourself, choose one of the selected entities to be the parent of the others. Once you have decided which entity will be the parent and have created the parent-child relationship between the entities, attempt to make the slice again, and the "Cannot Create Slice" message window will no longer appear, as a single transform root will have been defined.

Slices are not only a great way to group together entities into a single asset object, they also can contain instances of other slices. When experimenting with slice creation, I urge you to create a slice that contains an instance of at least one other slice.

Instantiating Slices

To utilize slices that exist within your project's directory, we will need to learn how to load instances of these slices into our project level. This process of loading instances of slices is also known as "instantiating" slices. There are three ways to instantiate slices.

If your viewport's camera is positioned in a location that you would like for a slice to be instantiated, click and drag a slice asset from the Asset Browser window onto the viewport. The slice will be instantiated at the location at which you release the click.

The second way of instantiating a slice is by right-clicking in the viewport to display the select menu. Select the "Instantiate Slice" option from the pop-up list. The "Pick Slice" dialog box will appear, allowing you to navigate to the slice file to instantiate. Once the slice is selected, click the "OK" button in the bottom right-hand corner of the window, and the slice will have been instantiated.

The third and final way of instantiating a slice is similar to the second method; however, instead of right-clicking in the viewport area to display the select menu, we will right-click an area inside of the Entity Outliner window to display the same menu. Selecting the "Instantiate Slice" option from the pop-up list will load the same "Pick Slice" dialog box as option two offered up and following the same steps as option two will yield the same result.

Creating Your Player

Let us experiment with this by instantiating our first slice into Amazon Lumberyard. The engine provides a player character slice that we can use in our game that will allow us to get a head start in our game development process. Keep in mind that because slices are modifiable, this character slice can be given a new skin, new physics components, new sound effects, and more.

To instantiate your character player slice, right-click an area within the Entity Outliner window and select the "Instantiate slice..." button to open the "Pick Slice" dialog box. In the search bar, type "PlayerSlice_EFX" to reveal the slice file that exists within the MyFirstGame/Slices directory, as shown in Figure 5-7.

Figure 5-7. *The playerslice_efx.slice file is a character player slice provided by Amazon Lumberyard that we can use to kick-start our game project*

You will notice that when clicking the "Play Game" button, your character will not be controllable at this point. This is due to the slice components missing some files that we did not copy over from the StarterGame folder. We did not copy them over on purpose, as in Chapter 6 when we discuss components, we will get some hands-on experience with creating the components ourselves.

Now that your character has been added to the game, we need to add some props for our character to interact with. Amazon Lumberyard provides a great deal of prop-like slices that we can use to spruce up our game. Take some time before moving on to the next chapter to initiate some prop-slices from the MyFirstGame/Slices folder and create a world for your character to explore, as shown in Figure 5-8.

Figure 5-8. *Amazon Lumberyard provides many slices you can use as building blocks to learn how to create games and to jump-start your game development journey*

Keep in mind that if all of your entities and slices that are dropped into your viewport or instantiated via the Entity Outliner window have a mesh consisting of only gray squares, your Project Configurator may not have copied the necessary materials over from the StarterGame directory, so you may need to do this manually.

Copy the "Materials" folder from the StarterGame project directory, located at

```
C:\Amazon\Lumberyard\<Lumberyard_Version>\dev\StarterGame\
Materials
```

Once you have the "Materials" folder in your clipboard, navigate to your MyFirstGame directory, located at

```
C:\Amazon\Lumberyard\<Lumberyard_Version>\dev\MyFirstGame\
```

Once you have navigated to the MyFirstGame directory, use the keyboard key-command Ctrl+V to paste the folder into your MyFirstGame directory.

If the meshes do not update on your assets immediately, restart Amazon Lumberyard and the changes should be reflected.

Now that you have a firm understanding of what entities and slices are, you have your own character created, and you have props for your character to interact with, it is time to breathe life into your character. In Chapter 6 we will discuss entity components so we can control our character and learn the necessary skills to create adventurous levels.

CHAPTER 6

Components

Entities make up the core content of an entire game project in Amazon Lumberyard, but components are arguably the most important thing you need to know about when creating a game – as they are what make entities come to life. Entities in Amazon Lumberyard are merely identifiers that link to a collection of components. Entities have no functionality associated with them on their own – their functionality comes from the components added to them.

Components in Lumberyard will each provide independent functionality for things like artificial intelligence, gameplay, physics, environment, and more. Keep in mind that some components will only be available through gems, so after reading through this chapter, it may behoove you to open your Project Configurator and scroll through some optional components you might like to experiment with.

Adding Components to an Entity

To add a component to an entity, right-click the entity and select the "Open Pinned Inspector" option from the menu that pops up. Click the "Add Component" button directly above the list of components, as shown in Figure 6-1.

© Jaken Chandler Herman 2019
J. C. Herman, *Beginning Game Development with Amazon Lumberyard*,
https://doi.org/10.1007/978-1-4842-5073-0_6

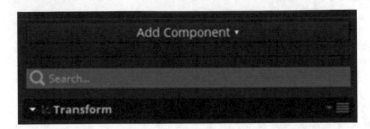

Figure 6-1. *Click the "Add Component" button in the entity Pinned Inspector window to add components to entities*

Once you've clicked the "Add Component" button, a list of all available components will appear with a search bar, allowing you to search for and find a specific component quickly if you know the name of the component already.

The component list will be grouped by the category in which the component belongs. I will briefly give a description of what each component is; however, I will only go in depth about components that we will be using in our project. Keep in mind by the time of your reading this text, more components may exist, but the ones I detail will likely still remain.

To start, let us look at what AI components are available for our use.

AI Components

Behavior Tree	Loads and runs Modular Behavior Tree references on the selected entity. Modular Behavior Trees, or MBTs, are collections of ideas for creating what behavior your artificial intelligent entities in your game should do. Without writing any code, MBTs allow you to describe AI behaviors.
Navigation	Navigation is used on artificial intelligent entities for accepting navigation commands for pathfinding and following. This can be used in our game later on and will be discussed in more detail in Chapter 7.

(continued)

AI Components

Navigation Area	Navigation area allows you to add a constraint on which area of your game is navigable by your artificial intelligence.
Navigation Seed	Navigation seeds are used to fine-tune artificial intelligence accessibility. For example, if there is a large rock that an artificial intelligence could not climb that exists within the navigation area, you could exclude the rocky area from the navigation seed to mark that area as an inaccessible area.

The next group of components is the animation group.

Animation Components

Actor	The Actor component is used to create characters in your game. You must use an Actor component to create your controllable character in your game.
AnimGraph	AnimGraph is used to add animation graphs and motion sets to your player character. This must be used in tandem with an Actor component.
Attachment	This component is used to attach entities to a joint on the skeleton of another parent entity. For example, this is how we can attach a weapon to our player character, as we will see later in the chapter.
Simple Motion	The Simple Motion component is used to play motions without the use of animation graph files.

The AnimGraph and Actor Components

Before moving onto the next group of components, let us take this time
to add some of these animation components that we will need to add to
our player character. We will also look at an interesting caveat that exists
between certain components along the way. The first component we
will need to add, as the preceding table states, is the "Actor" component.
However, because the AnimGraph component requires an Actor
component to exist on an entity, let us add the AnimGraph component
first to see what happens.

Right-click our player slice from the Entity Outliner window and select
the "Open Pinned Inspector" option. Click the "Add Component" button
that is shown in Figure 6-1, then in the search bar that appears, type
"AnimGraph" to filter the list of available components to only show the
AnimGraph component.

Select AnimGraph to add this component to our slice. As you will
notice in Figure 6-2, components that require other components to exist
on an entity will display a yellow triangle with an exclamation mark in
them with a warning message that states: *"This component is missing a
required component service and has been disabled."*

Below the warning message, there will be a button labeled "Add
Required Component" that will allow you to add any and all components
that must coexist with the component at hand. Click the "Add Required
Component" button now to show a list of all required components.
As we can see, the AnimGraph component only requires that an Actor
component also exists on the entity or slice, so click the "Actor" option now
to add the Actor component to our player character slice as well.

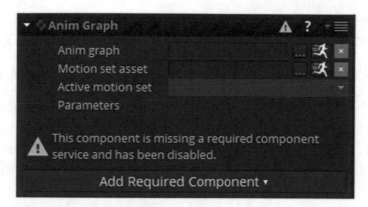

Figure 6-2. *Components that require other components will be disabled until all required components have been added to the entity or slice that they are being added to*

As you can tell from Figure 6-2, there are a few things that need to be linked up in the AnimGraph component in order to get the full functionality of the component. The first, the "Anim graph" field, will require you to locate a .ANIMGRAPH file on your computer, which holds animation graphs. These can be created and edited through the Animation Editor window; however, Amazon Lumberyard provides us with one we can use to get up and running quicker. Keep in mind that this animation graph may not be suitable for all characters you may create in your projects; however, it will provide a great reference for you to learn how to create your own animation graphs.

To locate this .ANIMGRAPH file, we first need to verify that the animations folder from the StarterGame project directory has been added to our MyFirstGame project directory, and if it has not, we need to copy it over at this point. First, navigate to the following location to check to see if a folder titled "animations" not only exists but is also not empty:

```
C:\Amazon\Lumberyard\<Lumberyard_Version>\dev\MyFirstGame
```

If the folder does not exist in the preceding directory or if the folder exists and is empty, navigate to the StarterGame project directory, located in

`C:\Amazon\Lumberyard\<Lumberyard_Version>\dev\StarterGame`

Select the animations folder, and use the keyboard key-combination Ctrl+C to copy the folder to your machine's clipboard. Now that you have the animations folder copied, go back to your MyFirstGame project directory and use the keyboard key-combination Ctrl+V to paste the animations folder to your directory.

While we are at it, let us go ahead and take the scripts, scriptcanvas, and libs folders as well. If you already have non-empty scripts, scriptcanvas, and libs folders in your MyFirstGame project directory, feel free to skip this step – but if you either do not have these folders, or the folders are empty, go to the StarterGame project directory located above, and copy the folders titled "Scripts," "scriptcanvas," as well as "libs" by selecting the folders and using the keyboard key-combination Ctrl+C.

Navigate back to your MyFirstGame directory, and paste the folders into your directory by using the keyboard key-combination Ctrl+V. Now that we have what we need for our Actor and AnimGraph components, we will restart our Amazon Lumberyard Editor.

Once your editor has restarted, we need to get back to the window where we could link up our animation graphs to our character slice, as was shown in Figure 6-2. Right-click our player slice from the Entity Outliner window and select the "Open Pinned Inspector" option.

You will notice to the right of each of the fields in the AnimGraph component there will be three options. The first option, whose icon is "...", allows you to browse through your file system to locate the .ANIMGRAPH file we just moved over into our project directory. The second option, whose icon is a running person, will open up the Animation Editor window. This would be useful if you did not have an existing .ANIMGRAPH file, as you can create one directly from the AnimGraph component. Keep in mind, if you already have an .ANIMGRAPH file linked to the AnimGraph component, clicking this button will open the Animation Editor window to allow you to edit the currently linked animation graph file. The next option is an "X," and it will allow you to clear any asset that is linked up in the AnimGraph component.

For now, we need to link our .ANIMGRAPH file, so we will select the "..." icon to the right of the "Anim graph" input which will open a window titled "Pick EMotion FX Anim Graph." From this window, search for "JackAnimGraph.animgraph", and select the asset whose name matches the search criteria. Select the orange "OK" button in the bottom right-hand corner of the window to link this .ANMIGRAPH file to our AnimGraph component.

The next field we need to fill out is the "Motion set asset" field. Select the "..." icon to locate the .motionset file we just moved over from the StarterGame directory, and a window will appear titled "Pick EMotion FX Motion Set." In the search bar of this window, type "JackMotionSet.motionset", and select the asset whose name matches the search criteria. Click the orange "OK" button in the bottom right-hand corner to link the .motionset asset to our AnimGraph component's "Motion set asset" field.

Once the motion set asset is applied to the component, you will notice that the "Active motion set" input will be prefilled with the newly added .motionset asset, and we can now make modifications to the parameters on the AnimGraph component. These parameters include things like "Speed," "CanDoubleJump," "TurnSpeed," and more. For now, I will opt to leave these parameters alone; however, I encourage you to tinker with them to make your character's motion set unique.

Because our AnimGraph component required an Actor component, all we need to do now is link the actor asset that we moved over from the StarterGame project directory to the Actor component.

To do this, in the "Actor asset" input on the Actor component, click the "..." icon to open a window titled "Pick EMotion FX Actor." In the search bar, type "Jack," and select the option titled "jack (EMotion FX Actor)," then select the orange "OK" button in the bottom right-hand corner of the screen. The actor asset will now be linked to our Actor component.

If you click the "Play Game" button, you will now be able to control your character. W to move forward, S to move backward, A to move left, D to move right, and spacebar to jump. You can also connect a gamepad like a PlayStation or Xbox controller to control your character as well. Later in the chapter, we will look at how you can make changes to what buttons control certain aspects of your character, but for now, we will move on to the next component.

The Attachment Component

As stated in the table for the Animation group of components, the attachment component is used to attach entities to a joint on the skeleton of another parent entity. Our player slice contains a "PlasmaRifle" slice that I would like to attach to the right hand of our character "Jack." To do this, right-click the "PlasmaRifle" slice in the Entity Outliner window and select the "Open Pinned Inspector" option, then select the "Add Component" button. Search for "Attachment" in the search bar that appears, and select the component that pops up.

An attachment component will now be added to our PlasmaRifle slice; now all we need to do is tell the component which entity we would like it to attach to. Because I am right-handed, I would like to attach the rifle to Jack's right hand, but feel free to attach it to his left. To do so, in the "Target entity" input on the attachment component, select the crosshair logo, then select Jack either in the viewport or in the Entity Outliner window. Selecting the crosshair logo allows you to choose which entity you would like to attach to without having to dig through a list of entities in the Entity Outliner list – you can just do it through the viewport.

Now that Jack is selected as the target entity for our attachment component, we need to specify which of Jack's joints we would like to attach to. In the "Joint name" input, select the drop-down menu to display a list of all possible joints. Again, I will be selecting the right hand, so I will choose the option titled "Jack:r_hand".

Below the Target entity and Joint name inputs, you do have the option to offset the position, rotation, and scale of the PlasmaRifle slice, but the defaults are sufficient in our case. After the offset inputs, we have the option to set the PlasmaRifle to be attached initially or not. If you would not like your character to start with a weapon, you can un-click this value; however, I would like to get into the action as fast as I can, so I will opt to leave the "Attached initially" option selected.

Once your weapon is attached to Jack, your attachment component should look like Figure 6-3. To verify that your weapon looks good on your character and that no position, rotation, or scaling offsets are needed, click the "Play Game" button to inspect your handiwork.

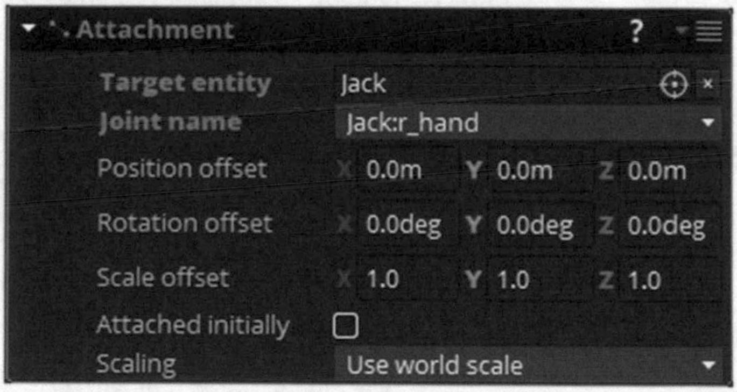

Figure 6-3. *The attachment component allows you to attach entities and slices to other entities and slices*

Now that we have successfully made it through all of the animation components, let us take a look at the next group of available components – the audio components. Because we will cover audio in depth in a later chapter, I will define what each component does but will not show examples as these components will be utilized in a further chapter.

Audio Components

Audio Area Environment	Allows you to apply environment effects to sounds that entities trigger.
Audio Environment	Used to apply environmental effects like echoing or reverberation.
Audio Listener	Only one audio listener per game is allowed. This component will place a simulated microphone in the environment.
Audio Preload	Allows you to load and unload Audio Transition Layer preloads either automatically or manually.
Audio Proxy	Required if multiple audio components are added to an entity.
Audio RTPC	Provides real-time parameter control capabilities. RTPCs are variables that can be set at run time to provide the capability to tweak sounds in-game.
Audio Switch	Provides ATL switch functionality, which allows you to specify that different sounds can come out of different entities. For example, a "GroundType" switch could have different audio values for grass, gravel, and water.
Audio Trigger	Provides play/stop features that can be executed on demand when an in-game action occurs.

The next group of components to choose from in the Pinned Inspector window are the Camera components, which only consist of two simple components:

Camera Components

Camera	This component should be used on entities that will be used as cameras. To use this component, you must have the "Camera Framework Gem" enabled on your project.
Camera Rig	Used to modify behaviors to drive your camera entity. This component also requires the "Camera Framework Gem" be enabled on your project.

In our player slice, we have a camera entity that has a camera component attached to it already. We are going to modify this component, however, to increase our field of view for our camera from the default 45.0 degrees to 75.0 degrees.

To do this, right-click the camera entity in the Entity Outliner that exists within our player slice, and select the "Open Pinned Inspector" option. Either scroll down until you find the camera component, or search "Camera" in the search bar beneath the "Add Component" button. In the input labeled "Field of view," change the default text from 45.0 to 75.0. This will allow us to see more of what is going on in the game when walking around our world with our character. Your camera component should now match Figure 6-4.

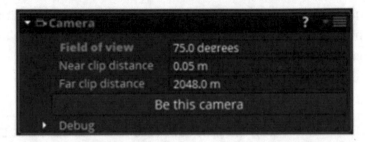

Figure 6-4. *The camera component should be added to entities that will be used as in-game cameras*

You may also notice that this camera entity has many Lua scripts associated. We will modify these when we introduce Lua scripting in Chapter 8.

The next component group available to choose from in the Pinned Inspector is the "Editor" group, which only contains a single component.

Editor Components

Comment	The comment component is strictly for you, the developer. It will allow you to add a comment to an entity that will not have any effect on in-game content. Think of this as a way of keeping notes within entities.

The next component group also only contains one component. This is a component that we will be using to add another level of detail and professionalism to our game.

Environment Components

Fog Volume	The Fog Volume component is used to create a fog-like effect within your game. This component must be used in tandem with the Box Shape component.

The Fog Volume Component

Let us add some fog to our game. I will opt to create fog directly where my player character is standing, and keep in mind that this is something that you can do to match your taste on your own, so our outcomes for fog will be different. You may like yours a different color or perhaps denser, and that is okay. I will create a green fog around my character as if it were some sort of noxious gas. My character is currently in a maze I created from entities that Amazon Lumberyard provides, and now I will add green foggy gas all in the maze area to make it seem like my character must escape some lab accident gone wrong.

To do this, we first need to add a new entity to our game to hold the Fog Volume component. Right-click in the Entity Outliner window and select "Create Entity." Now right-click the empty new entity and select "Open Pinned Inspector." Select the "Add component" button, then search "Fog Volume" in the search bar and select the option that pops up. Alternatively, you can scroll to the "Environment" section of the components list and select the Fog Volume component that way.

Once the Fog Volume component has been added to your entity, as stated in the preceding table, and as you will notice on the Fog Volume component within your game, the Box Shape component is a required counterpart, so we need to add this component now. At the bottom of the Fog Volume component area in the Pinned Inspector, click the button labeled "Add Required Component," followed by the sole "Box Shape" option that pops up.

On the Fog Volume component, we are going to change a few properties while leaving some of them at their default settings. I highly recommend you tinker with all of the properties on the Fog Volume component to see what they do and to experiment with them, but for the purposes of this text, we will only be changing a few properties.

The first property we will change is "Volume type," which can either be an ellipsoid or cuboid. This merely specifies the shape of the fog, and because my maze is rectangular and I want the entire maze area to be filled, I will choose the cuboid volume type. To do this, click the drop-down menu for volume type and select "Cuboid".

The next property I will change is going to be the "Color" property, which allows you to specify the color of the fog via a color picker that is attached. Because I want my fog to represent a green noxious gas, I will change the color to RGB 0, 255, 0. To do this, click the white square next to the "Color" input, and a color picker will pop up. Feel free to choose a gray, red, blue, or any other color you want to make your game unique. Also, keep in mind that in the Time of Day Editor, you can set a global fog color as well as other global fog properties. If you already have a global color defined in the Time of Day Editor, you can choose to check the input box for the "Use global fog color" option in the Fog Volume component. If this box is selected, any value in the color field of the component will be ignored, and the global Time of Day fog color will be used.

The last property we will change on this component is the "Fog Density." I do not want fog so thick that my character would not be able to see through it, so I will change this option to 0.01 by typing in the input box next to the fog density input label.

Now that I have my fog set up, I just need to use the transform tools we described in Chapter 2 to make the fog area match the space and size of my maze. Take time now to get your fog to the size, space, color, and density that you would like it to be for your game. This will add an extra level of quality to your game.

When you have finished this step, your Fog Volume component should look something like the left side of Figure 6-5, and your game should look similar to the right side of Figure 6-5, with minor differences in fog color, density, vegetation patters, and choice of entities used to create an area for your character to interact with.

Figure 6-5. *The Fog Volume component allows you to add fog or gas to your game environment, as shown in the photo on the right. In the photo on the left, we see some of the modifiable properties of the Fog Volume component.*

Now that our game has a nice, professional touch to it, let us take a look at the next available component group – the gameplay group.

Gameplay Components

Input	The input component allows you to set key bindings, mouse bindings, and game controller bindings for input events in your game.
Random Timed Spawner	The Random Time Spawner component allows you to spawn a slice at a specified interval to a random position inside specified boundaries. We will look at this further in Chapter 7.
Simple State	This component allows you to create a simple state machine.
Spawner	Allows you to spawn slices, whether design-time or dynamic at an entity's location.
Tag	The tag component allows you to apply labels, also known as "tags," to an entity. These tags can be used to filter and target entities with certain traits.

The next component group, the "Networking" group only contains a single component.

Networking Components

Network Binding	This component allows you to specify whether or not an entity is able to be replicated across the network.

The next component group is the Physics component group.

Physics Components

Character Physics	Adds physical behaviors to character entities (players and enemies).
Constraint	Creates physical constraints between an entity and its target.
Force Volume	This component is used to apply physical force to objects.
Mesh Collider	The mesh collider component allows you to define the shape that collision detection will take place in.
Primitive Collider	A simple collider that is used with a shape component for collision detection.
Rigid Body Physics	This component should be used to represent solid objects that move realistically when interacted with.
Static Physics	This component should be used to represent unmovable objects like walls or boundaries.
Wind Volume	The wind volume component creates volumes that are affected by wind, which should be used to affect vegetation and other physical objects.

The Wind Volume Component

To add wind to our game, let us create an entity and add the wind volume component to that entity. We have to keep in mind that the wind volume component must be used with either a Box Shape component or a Sphere Shape component.

To begin, right-click inside the Entity Outliner window, then choose the option "Create Entity." Once your entity has been created, right-click the entity, then choose "Open Pinned Inspector." In the name field, change the default entity name to "Wind," so we will be able to identify this entity later on.

Next, click the "Add Component" button, then type "Wind Volume" to narrow the search results down to only the wind volume component, then choose the wind volume component to add it to your entity.

When your wind volume component is added to your wind entity, the component will be disabled by default, as it will be missing a required component service. To add the required component, select the "Add Required Component" button, followed by either "Box Shape" or "Sphere Shape" – whichever one you choose is up to you.

To set the area that the wind will affect, change the dimensions of your shape in the dimensions area of the component. For my game, I will set a fairly small area to be windy – and I have chosen to use a Box Shape component, so I will set my X, Y, and Z dimensions to be 5.0 meters each.

Now that I have an area for the wind to affect, we can set some of the properties on the wind volume component. First, make sure that the "Visible" property is checked so we can actually see the wind and so that it will interact with the vegetation of your game. The next property is the "Falloff" property, which will affect the speed of the wind from the center of the entity to the edge of the shape component's volume. Set this property to 0.5 by either typing the value into the input box next to the "Falloff" label or by using the slider to the right of the input box.

The next property we can change is the speed property, which obviously will allow you to set the speed of the wind. Feel free to set your wind speed to whatever you would like, depending on how windy you would like your game area to be. I would like mine to be extremely windy, so I will set the speed to 40 m/s.

The next property, air resistance, will cause objects moving through the windy area to slow down. Set this value to whatever you would like. For my example, I will set this property to 5.0. After air resistance is air density. Objects with lower density will rise, while objects with a higher density will sink. Set this value to whatever you would like. Once again, for my example, I will set this property to 5.0.

Finally, we need to define the direction of the wind in meters per second along the box shape's axes. To create an omnidirectional wind, you can leave the values for all three axes, X, Y, and Z, to 0. For my example, I will leave these values at 0 for an omnidirectional wind. When you have finished adding the wind volume component, it will look something like Figure 6-6.

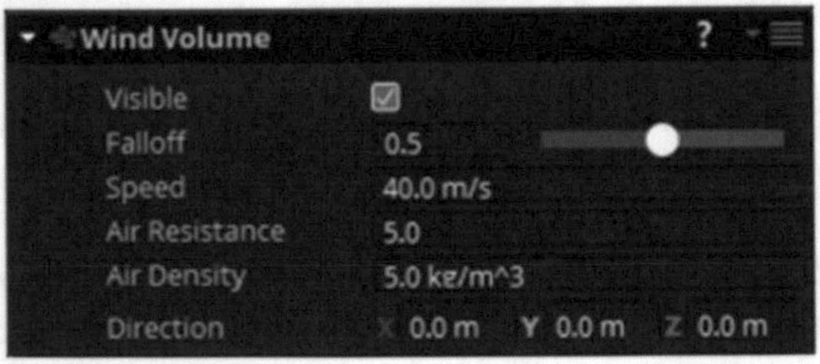

Figure 6-6. *The wind volume component allows you to add wind to your game alongside a Box Shape or Sphere Shape component*

Now that we have added wind to our game, let us move on to the next component group, the rendering group.

Rendering Components

Area Light	Use this component to light an area.
Decal	Used to place a component on an entity, given a decal material file.
Environment Probe	This component is used to achieve a proper visual quality for a given space.
Geometry Cache	This component will render mesh data and can be used to play animations from Alembic files, which is a type of computer graphics interchange framework.
High Quality Shadow	This component can be used to give an entity its own shadow map that will allow you to achieve a higher resolution shadow than you would get with a global shadow map.
Lens Flare	This component allows you to place a lens flare on an entity.
Mesh	The mesh component should be used to add visual geometry to and entity.
Particle	This component will place a particle emitter on an entity. Entities can have more than 1 particle components.
Point Light	This component will create a point of light.
Projector Light	This component will project light when added to an entity.

CHAPTER 6   COMPONENTS

The Particle Component

Another level of detail we can add to our game that will make it stand out as a professional development is a particle emitter. Amazon Lumberyard provides us with a particle emitter that is actually a flock of flying birds. Let us add some birds to our game now.

To begin, right-click inside the Entity Outliner window, then choose the option "Create Entity." Once your entity has been created, right-click the entity, then choose "Open Pinned Inspector." In the name field, change the default entity name to "Birds," so we will be able to identify this entity later on.

Next, click the "Add Component" button, then search "Particle" to narrow down the search results. Select "Particle" to add a particle component to our new "Birds" entity. To the right of the "Particle effect library," you will see an icon with three dots. When you click this button, a new window will appear titled "Pick Particles."

The particle XML file we would like to use is located in MyFirstGame\libs\particles. Navigate through the directory to find birds.xml, or just search "birds.xml" in the search bar at the top of the window. Select the birds.xml file, then click the orange "OK" button in the bottom right-hand corner of the window.

In the "Emitters" property drop-down box, select "Birds.BirdsFlying," and make sure that both the "Visible" and "Enable" properties are checked. Your game will now have birds flying around. Keep in mind, if you would like your game to be more saturated, you can add more than one particle component to an entity.

Once you have added the particle component to your entity, your component will look something like Figure 6-7.

140

Figure 6-7. *The particle component can be used to add another level of detail to your game by adding a particle emitter*

Let us move on to the next component group, the scripting group.

Scripting Components

Lua Script	Add programming logic to an entity in the form of a Lua script. We will use these in Chapter 8.
Script Canvas	This component can be used to add a script to an entity.
Trigger Area	This component provides standard triggering services in tandem with shape components as its boundaries.

The final component group we will discuss will be the user interface component group.

UI Components

UI Canvas Asset Ref	This component allows you to associate a UI canvas with an entity in a level.
UI Canvas Proxy Ref	This component allows you to associate an entity in a level with a different entity that is managing a UI canvas.
UI Canvas on Mesh	The component lets you place a UI canvas on an entity in the world that your player can interact with.

For now, we will not worry about adding any of the UI components, as all of our user interface work will be added in Chapter 10.

The Transform Component

As mentioned briefly in Chapter 5, the transform component, shown in Figure 6-8, will exist on every entity you create by default. The transform component does not belong to any component group, it merely exists on its own. The transform component will store all values for scaling, rotation, and translations, as well as information about which entity is the parent entity of the currently inspected entity, if any parent entity exists. If you have skipped ahead to this chapter and are unfamiliar with parent-child entity relationships, I would highly recommend going back and reading Chapter 5 of this book.

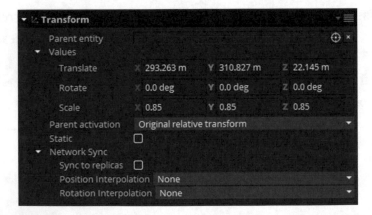

Figure 6-8. *The transform component will exist on every entity that is created within Amazon Lumberyard*

As stated previously in Chapter 5, we can essentially "create" a child entity from an existing entity by clicking the reticle icon next to the "Parent entity" field on the entity inspector. Once this button has been selected, we need to choose which entity we would like to be the parent by either selecting its name from the list of entities in the Entity Outliner window or by selecting the entity directly from the viewport. By selecting a parent entity for the currently inspected entity, Amazon Lumberyard will create a reference link between the two entities to add the parent-child relationship.

If your entity has a parent entity and you would like to remove the reference to the parent entity from the inspector window, select the "X" button to the right of the reticle icon you just used. By clicking this button, Amazon Lumberyard will remove the reference link between the two entities, making them independent of one another.

Now that we have added multiple components to our game and to our player character, it is time to create someone for our character to interact with – the enemy. In the next chapter, we will look at creating our first enemy.

CHAPTER 7

Creating the Enemy

Now that we have learned all about entities and components, let us take a look at how we can tie in these concepts to create an enemy for our player character. We will look at how to do this using two different methods.

The first method we will explore will be to just create an enemy entity from a preexisting slice provided by Amazon Lumberyard that will exist from the minute you click the "Play Game" button in the editor.

The second method will be to utilize the use of enemy spawners, AI navigators, and AI triggers. Keep in mind, all of the artwork and scripting for the enemy character that we will use will be the assets that are provided for us by the Amazon Lumberyard engine.

Ready to have an evil robotic enemy that your player character must tiptoe around the maze with, ready to defeat your character mercilessly on sight? Let's go!

Creating an Enemy That Always Exists

To begin, let us create an enemy that does not rely on spawners or patrol areas within your game. This enemy will merely stand in place until your character comes into sight, then they will attack.

To do this, instantiate a slice either by right-clicking in the viewport or the Entity Outliner window and selecting the option "Instantiate slice." In the window that appears labeled "Pick Slice," navigate to the slice named

© Jaken Chandler Herman 2019
J. C. Herman, *Beginning Game Development with Amazon Lumberyard*,
https://doi.org/10.1007/978-1-4842-5073-0_7

`ai_walker_efx.slice`, which is provided by Amazon Lumberyard. This slice will be located in the directory `MyFirstGame/slices`. Alternatively, you can use the search bar at the top of the "Pick Slice" window and search for `ai_walker_efx`. Select the slice, then click the orange "OK" button in the bottom right-hand corner of the window. Your slice will now have been added to your game.

Another way we could have added this slice to our game is by opening the Asset Browser by selecting "Tools" in the top menu bar, followed by "Asset Browser." Once the Asset Browser is open, navigate to the `ai_walker_efx.slice` file, or enter it into the search bar at the top of the Asset Browser. Click and drag the slice into the viewport to add the enemy to your game.

When you click the "Play Game" button and navigate your character to the area in which this enemy is standing, the enemy will open fire and try to diminish your life points. While it is a good start, this is not the best way to implement an enemy into your game. Let us take a look at another method of adding enemies.

Creating an Enemy AI Trigger

For our enemy artificial intelligence to spawn in an appropriate location at an appropriate time, we need to set up some boundaries that will trigger the spawner to activate. When our player character enters the area, the spawner will be triggered and our enemy will be spawned.

To begin, we need to add the debug manager provided by Amazon Lumberyard into our list of entities. This slice will manage some of the artificial intelligence script's functional behavior. This slice is located in `MyFirstGame/Slices`.

Open the Asset Browser by selecting "Tools" in the top menu bar, followed by "Asset Browser." Once selected, this should add another panel on the side of the viewport (or add a new window). Once the Asset Browser is open, search for `debug_manager.slice`, or navigate to it under MyFirstGame/Slices. Drag the debug_manager.slice file into the viewport to add it to the game.

Now that the debug manager has been added to the game, we need to add our trigger entity. In the Entity Outliner window or in the viewport area, right-click and choose the option "Create entity." Once the entity has been created, right-click it and select the option "Open Pinned Inspector." Rename the entity "AiTrigger," so we will know which entity in our Entity Outliner list holds our AI trigger later on. You can name it anything you want, but I recommend sticking with "AiTrigger" for tutorial purposes.

Before adding the trigger area component to our AiTrigger entity, we need to specify the boundaries of the trigger. To do this, we need to add a Box Shape component to our entity. To do so, click the "Add Component" button, and search for "Box Shape" in the search bar. Click the "Box Shape" component to add it to our AiTrigger entity. Once the Box Shape component has been added to the entity, we need to specify the dimensions. Because I would like to have a nice tall area that we can both see when editing and trigger when playing as our character, let us set the X and Y dimensions to 20 meters each and the Z dimension to 10 meters. To do this, type the size values in each of the corresponding x-, y-, and z-axis inputs to the right of the "Dimensions" label.

When we are setting up our trigger area, it would be best if we could see the area in which we are setting the trigger. To enable the area visibility, make sure the checkbox next to the "Visible" label in the Box Shape component is checked. Because we do not want our player character to know where the boundaries of the trigger area are, make sure the checkbox next to the "Game View" label in the Box Shape component is unchecked.

Use the move tool in the EditMode toolbar to position the trigger area in a location that you think would be best for your game. You should be able to see the area as in Figure 7-1. If you are unable to see the box area in your viewport, click the ? icon in the upper right-hand corner of the viewport ().

Figure 7-1. *The Box Shape component is used here to create the boundaries for our AI trigger area*

When positioning the Box Shape component, be aware that the player controller needs to start outside of the AI trigger area in order to activate the spawner. If the game starts with the player character inside the boundaries of the trigger area, the player will need to leave the area, then reenter the area to trigger the AI. For my game, I have placed the AI trigger area just to the right of my player character, so if my player makes a right turn through my maze, it will activate the AI trigger, and the spawner will toggle (once we add it).

Now that we have our boundaries created, we can add the trigger area component to our AiTrigger entity. Click the "Add Component" button, then under "Scripting," choose "Trigger Area," or just type "Trigger Area" in the search bar. Click "Trigger Area" to add the component to the entity. Now, in the trigger area component, under the label "Tag Filters," click the "+" button next to the "Required tags" label. A new "Required tag" element will be added to the "Required tags" list under "Tag Filters." In the input area next to the label "[0]," type "PlayerCharacter." Your trigger area component should look like Figure 7-2.

148

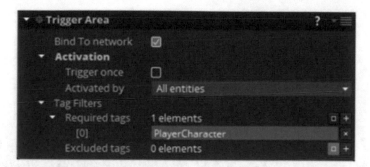

Figure 7-2. *The trigger area component for your AiTrigger entity should contain a required tag "PlayerCharacter"*

Next, we need to add the Lua script provided by Amazon Lumberyard that will trigger the AI spawn. In the next chapter, we will look at how to modify Lua scripts and create scripts of our own, but for now, let us just use the scripts we have provided. To add a Lua script to our AiTrigger entity, click the "Add Component" button, then under "Scripting," click "Lua Script," or just query for "Lua Script" in the search bar. Click "Lua Script" to add the component to the entity.

Once the Lua script component has been added to the entity, we need to link up the correct script to the entity. Next to the area labeled "Script," click the browse button, denoted by the icon with three horizontal dots.

A new window will pop up titled "Pick Lua Script," then choose the AISpawnTrigger.lua file. The file will be located under MyFirstGame/ Scripts/AI/AISpawnTrigger.lua, or you can just search for "AISpawnTrigger.lua" in the search bar of the "Pick Lua Script" window. Select the file, then click the orange "OK" button in the bottom right-hand corner of the screen. Now, under the "Properties" area in the "Lua Script" component, type "Group0" into the "AISpawnGroup" input box. Your scripts component should look like Figure 7-3.

Figure 7-3. *The AISpawnGroup should be set to Group0, and the Lua Script "Script" property should be set to AISpawnTrigger.lua for our AiTrigger entity*

Now when your player character enters the trigger area defined by the Box Shape component on our AiTrigger entity, the AI scripts in the group will be activated. When the player character leaves the box shape boundaries, the scripts will be deactivated.

Creating an Enemy AI Navigation Area

We have now defined an area in which the player will trigger the AI spawner for the enemy to appear when the player character gets too close. Now, we need to provide an AI navigation area, which is the area that is traversable for all artificially intelligent characters. Think of this as the boundaries in which the enemies can move through. AI characters will use this AI navigation area to find their way through the play space of the game.

The first thing we need to do is add an entity by right-clicking in either the Entity Outliner window or the viewport and selecting the option "Create entity." Once the entity is created, right-click the entity and select the option "Open Pinned Inspector." Once the Pinned Inspector is opened, we need to give this entity a name.

In the input field directly to the right of the label "Name," type "AiNavigationArea." Now, on our AiNavigationArea entity, we need to add the navigation area component. To do so, click the "Add Component" button in the Pinned Inspector for the AiNavigationArea entity. Under the

AI component group, select Navigation Area, or just search "Navigation Area" in the search bar, then select the component "Navigation Area" to add the component to your entity.

Because a polygon prism shape component is required for the navigation area to work, the navigation area component will be disabled by default. In the component, click the button "Add Required Component," followed by "Polygon Prism Shape."

Right-click your AiNavigationArea entity within the Entity Outliner window, then select "Find in Viewport" to zoom into the newly created component. If your setup has been done correctly up to this point, your entity should look similar to Figure 7-4.

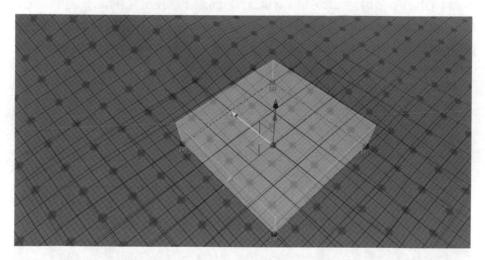

Figure 7-4. *The initial setup of the AI Navigation Area component entity should look similar to this photo when first created*

In the Pinned Inspector for your AiNavigationArea entity, inside the Navigation Area component we have just added to the entity, click the + icon to the far right of the "Agent Types" label to add a new agent type to the component. The new agent type you have just added will have a label of "[0]" and a drop-down box to the right of it. Click the drop-down box, and choose the option "MediumSizedCharacters."

Now let us focus our attention to the polygon prism shape component – specifically the height. We need to make the height a large enough area for our AI characters to explore. In the input box to the right of the "Height" label, change the value to 5.0 meters instead of the default 1.0 meters.

To be able to see the defined path data for AI navigation, we need to set the MediumSizedCharacters view agent type property to be "true." To do this, navigate to the very top of Amazon Lumberyard in the menu bar, and select the "Game" menu, followed by the "AI" menu. In the AI menu, navigate to the "View Agent Type" menu, and select "MediumSizedCharacters" (once selected, a blue check mark will appear next to the option). A blue box will now appear within the navigation area that you have created. The AI characters will use this blue section to define path data to move around in the game space. If done correctly, your entity will now appear like the one in Figure 7-5.

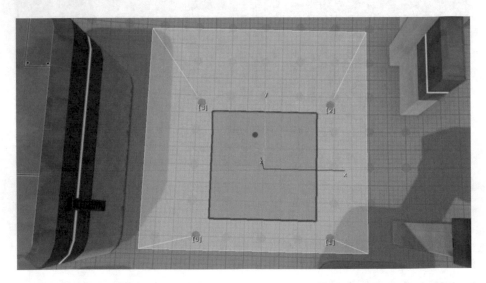

Figure 7-5. *The blue area allows you to visualize the path data for AI characters*

Next, we need to align our AI navigation area entity to another object in order to make it easier for us to create a walkable path. Because my game example is set up as a maze of sorts, I will align my AI navigation area entity to one of my walls in a corner.

Note   If the blue box does not appear in your game, try using the keyboard key-command Ctrl + E simultaneously, or navigate to the menu bar, select "Game," and "Export to Engine."

To do this, first make sure the Object toolbar is visible by right clicking the toolbar area. If the "Object Toolbar" option does not have a check mark beside it, select this option now. If this option does have a check mark beside it, your object toolbar is already visible. Select the "Align to object" button on the object toolbar ( ), then click the wall or other entity you would like to align the navigation area to.

Once your navigation area is aligned to an object, select the entity, and you will see that the corners of the entity are red and labeled in increasing numeric order from 0 to 3. Select and drag each vertex to create a perimeter of the area in which you would like your AI to be able to navigate through. When you have completed this step, your entity should now look something like Figure 7-6. Make sure your AiNavigationArea entity is lowered all the way to the ground so that path information will be defined. If path information is not defined, your enemy artificial intelligence characters will have nowhere to be able to roam. You can verify that your entity is touching the ground by the blue area defining the path data.

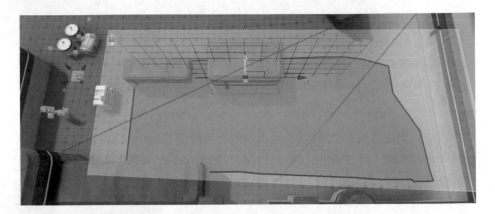

Figure 7-6. *Drag the red vertices on your Navigation Area component to set the navigation area to be larger. Make sure the blue area appears in your viewport, as this is how enemy artificial intelligence will determine path data.*

As you will likely notice, my path has two walls inside the walkable area. If my enemy were able to walk around my entire maze and game, there would be many elements that would potentially get in the way of my enemy's walking. However, because the blue path tells the enemy artificial intelligence that the wall is a viable, walkable path, my AI can try to walk in this area and has potential to get stuck.

To prevent this, select any entities within your walkable path, then right-click them, and select the option "Open Pinned Inspector." Next, look in the transform component of that entity, and enable the "Static" property, as shown in Figure 7-7. This will tell the navigation AI that the space these entities take up should not be included in the viable path options.

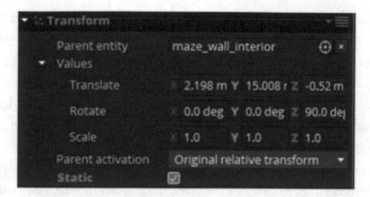

Figure 7-7. Static entities will be excluded from the viable path options for AI navigation areas

Creating an Enemy AI Spawn Point

We have our trigger for when it should happen, we have created the area that the enemy can navigate through when it happens, now all we need is the actual spawn point that the enemy will propagate from. A spawn point defines the precise location that the enemy artificial intelligence will appear once our player character has entered our AI trigger perimeter.

To begin, we first need to create an entity by right-clicking inside either the Entity Outliner window or the viewport, then selecting the option "Create entity." Once our entity has been created, right-click it and select the option "Open Pinned Inspector."

Inside the Pinned Inspector window for our newly created entity, let us change the name of the entity to something meaningful like "AiSpawner1" by entering the name in the input box directly to the right of the "Name" label.

Now that we have our entity set up, we need to add the AI spawner component to it. Click the "Add Component" button within the entity's Pinned Inspector window. Navigate to the "Spawner" component, either by looking under the "Gameplay" component group or by searching for the component in the search box at the top of the screen. Next, click "Spawner" to add the component to your entity.

To declare which entity will spawn from this spawner component, we need to select the dynamic slice for enemy AI. This is provided to us by Amazon Lumberyard, but keep in mind that you will be able to use any slice you would like or any slice you create. For the sake of this text, I will use the provided entities. To the right of the input box that is beside the "Dynamic slice" label, click the icon with three dots in order to select the dynamic slice associated with the spawner.

When clicking this button, a window will appear titled "Pick Dynamic slice." Navigate to MyFirstGame\slices, then select the slice named "ai_slice.slice". Alternatively, you can search for "ai_slice.slice" in the search bar at the top of the "Pick Dynamic slice" window. With the slice select, click the orange "OK" button in the bottom right-hand corner of the window.

In order to ensure the AI slice is not spawned when the game begins, but rather when the player character enters the AI trigger area, make sure the "Spawn on activate" property is set to false by unchecking the checkbox next to the "Spawn on activate" label. The next property, "Destroy on deactivate," is up to you to decide. When your player character leaves the AI trigger area, if you would like the enemy AI to be destroyed, mark this checkbox. If you would like your AI enemy to persist after your character has left the AI trigger area, leave this checkbox unmarked. For my game, I think it would be best to destroy enemies when my player character leaves the trigger area, so I will set this value to true.

If you have set up your spawner component correctly up to this point, it should look similar to Figure 7-8.

Figure 7-8. *The spawner component should look similar to this photo if created correctly*

The spawner component is not the only needed component, however, to enable enemy AI spawn points. We also need to add a Lua script provided by Amazon Lumberyard. To begin, add the "Lua Script" component to your AiSpawer1 entity by clicking the "Add Component" button. Next, under the "Scripting" component group, click "Lua Script," or just search for "Lua Script" on the top of the "Add Component" window.

Once you have selected "Lua Script," the component will be added to your entity. To the right of the input box directly beside the "Script" label, click the button whose icon is three dots in order to browse for the script file you would like to add.

A new window will appear titled "Pick Lua Script." Navigate to MyFirstGame\Scripts\AI and select AISpawner.lua, or just search for AISpawner.lua in the search bar at the top of this window. With AISpawner.lua selected, click the orange "OK" button in the bottom right-hand corner of this window to link the script with our Lua script component.

You will likely notice that quite a few new property items are now available on the Lua script component. We will discuss why this happens in Chapter 8, but for now let us move on to modifying these properties to the necessary values required to continue.

In the input box directly to the right of the "GroupId" label, input the value "Group0," as we did in our AI trigger area's spawn group property. This will link the spawner component on our AiSpawner1 entity to the AiTrigger entity's Lua script component. This tells the trigger what group ID it should be spawning. If done correctly, your Lua script should look like Figure 7-9.

Figure 7-9. *The final Lua script component on your AiSpawner1 entity **must** have "Group0" in the group ID, or it must at least be named the same as your AiTrigger entity's spawn group property.*

Click the "Play Game" button, and walk your player character through your AI trigger area. If all of the steps were followed correctly, a killer enemy robot will appear ready to fight your player character in a match to the death.

Creating Enemy Patrol Waypoints

You may notice that when your player character enters the AI trigger area, the enemy artificial intelligence will spawn, but this enemy will not walk around and patrol the AI navigation area that we created in the navigation area section. In this section, we will learn how to add AI patrol points, which will define the path the enemy should walk along as it patrols our game area. To do this, we will need to place AI waypoints.

To begin, we first need to create an entity by right-clicking inside either the Entity Outliner window or the viewport, then selecting the option "Create entity." Once our entity has been created, right-click it and select the option "Open Pinned Inspector."

Inside the Pinned Inspector window for our newly created entity, let us change the name of the entity to something meaningful like "AiWaypoint1" by entering the name in the input box directly to the right of the "Name" label.

Because this entity will only represent one waypoint for our enemy AI to navigate through, we need to create another waypoint entity a short distance away from our AiWaypoint1 entity. Follow the preceding steps, but instead of naming the entity "AiWaypoint1," this time, name the entity "AiWaypoint2." Create two more waypoint entities, named "AiWaypoint3" and "AiWaypoint4," and make a patrol pattern similar to the one in Figure 7-10.

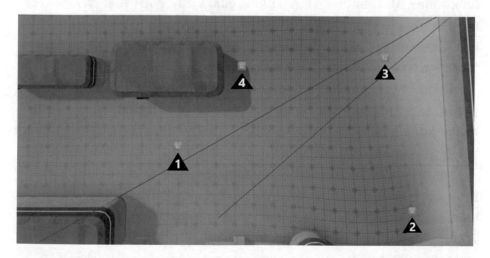

Figure 7-10. *Set up multiple AI waypoints for your enemy character to patrol. Make sure the waypoints are within the AI navigation area.*

Once you have your waypoints created for your enemy AI to navigate through, in your Entity Outliner window, right-click the entity we created in the last section named "AiSpawner1" and select the option "Open Pinned Inspector."

In the Pinned Inspector window for "AiSpawner1," click the "Add Component" button, and under the AI component group, select "Waypoints," or search for "Waypoints" in the search bar at the top of the window and select the "Waypoints" option that appears. Once you have selected "Waypoints," the component will be added to your "AiSpawner1" entity.

In the waypoint component area, make sure that the "Sentry?" and "Lazy Sentry?" properties are both unchecked. This will allow the enemy artificial intelligence to patrol between the waypoints you have created.

If the "Sentry?" property is selected, your enemy AI will stand in one place, turning occasionally to face different directions. This can be used for another AI enemy who is "standing guard" in a particular area, but for now, we want an enemy AI who *patrols*, so this needs to be unselected. If the "Lazy Sentry?" option is selected, the enemy AI will only look in the direction it faced when it was spawned.

In the "Waypoints" area of the waypoint component, click the "+" button seven times to add six waypoint elements to the component. The waypoints added will be labeled "[0]," "[1]," "[2]," "[3]," "[4]," "[5]," "[6}" with 7 empty inputs next to them.

The reason we added seven waypoint elements when we only have four waypoint entities is because we are defining the path they will walk along. In our case, we want our enemy to go from AiWaypoint1 to AiWaypoint2, then from AiWaypoint2 to AiWaypoint3, then AiWaypoint3 to AiWaypoint4. This is three waypoint routes; therefore, in order to have our enemy walk the path there and back, we need to specify seven waypoint elements in our waypoint component.

Click the "Pick" button next to the waypoint element input field labeled "[0]," which is denoted by a reticle icon 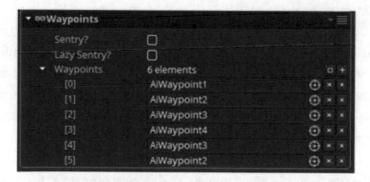, then select the "AiWaypoint1" entity in either the viewport or the Entity Outliner window. Do this for each waypoint element in the waypoint component in the following order: AiWaypoint1, AiWaypoint2, AiWaypoint3, AiWaypoint4, AiWaypoint3, AiWaypoint2, AiWaypoint1.

When this sequence is properly followed, this will cause our AI enemy to walk from our AiWaypoint1 to AiWaypoint2 to AiWaypoint3 to AiWaypoint4, at which point our enemy will turn around and walk from AiWaypoint4 to AiWaypoint3 to AiWaypoint2 and finally back to AiWaypoint1. Then, the sequence will restart, beginning with the first waypoint in the group. When your waypoints have all been selected in the waypoints component, your waypoints component should look similar to Figure 7-11.

Figure 7-11. *With waypoint elements defined, our enemy AI will navigate through the path we desire. Ensure that Sentry? and Lazy Sentry? are unchecked, or else the waypoint elements will be ignored.*

Keep in mind that when waypoints are not set, the enemy AI will operate in sentry mode regardless of whether or not the Sentry? or Lazy Sentry? properties are checked. This means our enemy would stand in their spawn point and turn periodically.

Click the "Play Game" button, and have your player character enter the AI trigger area we have defined. Now, your enemy will be patrolling the AI navigation area, so be careful not to get caught – or else.

Creating More AI Characters

To create more AI characters, follow all of the same preceding steps for the AI trigger area, AI navigation area, and the AI spawner. The only difference you will need to do is set up different waypoint areas, so your second AI enemy will patrol a different area of your game.

A quick way of having the trigger area, navigation area, and spawner settings to be replicated is to duplicate the first AI entities you have already created, then move them to a different location in the game. For my example, I will only duplicate the spawner and use the same navigation area and trigger area as my first AI spawn point uses.

To duplicate the AiSpawner1 entity, right-click the entity, then choose the option "Duplicate." By default, your newly duplicated entity will share a name with the parent entity from which it was created. Right-click this new entity, and choose the option "Open Pinned Inspector." In the input box directly to the right of the "Name" label, enter the name "AiSpawner2."

With the entity inspector still open for AiSpawner2, you will likely notice that all of the patrol waypoints were duplicated as well. Because we would like our second enemy to patrol a different area, or at least patrol via a new path, we need to clear all existing waypoints from our AiSpawner2 entity's waypoint component.

Directly to the right of the "Waypoints" label in the waypoints component, you will see another label that reads "7 elements." To the right of this label, there is a button whose icon is a square (). Clicking this square button will remove all existing waypoints from the AiSpawner2 entity. Do this now so we can create new waypoints for our new enemy.

Follow the steps in the previous section of this chapter to create waypoints for this new AiSpawner2 entity. Keep in mind you could create more, fewer, or the same number of waypoints for this new enemy to patrol through. For my game, I will only have my second enemy AI patrol an area with two waypoints, named "AiWaypoint5" and "AiWaypoint6." Using the "Move" tool, move the AiSpawner2 entity to an area within the AiNavigationArea different than where the AiSpawner1 currently occupies.

Tidying Up Our AI Entities

As you can likely tell, the more enemies we add, the more waypoints we will have. This can quickly muddy up our Entity Outliner window, and we may begin to confuse which AI waypoints and spawners belong to which AI enemy.

To remedy this, we will create parent entities for each of our enemies as well as a parent entity for all enemies as a group, because the navigation area and the trigger are shared.

To begin, right-click in the viewport or in the Entity Outliner window and select the "Create entity" option. This new entity will be the parent entity for the entities pertaining to the first enemy AI character. Right-click this new entity and select the option "Open Pinned Inspector." In the input box directly to the right of the "Name" label, input the value "Enemy 1."

Now, in the Entity Outliner window, hold down your Ctrl button on your keyboard, and select all entities relating to your first enemy artificial intelligence, excluding the AiTrigger and the AiNavigationArea. For my game example, these entities would be "AiSpawner1" and "AiWaypoint" entities number 1 through 4. When all of your first AI enemy associated entities are selected, drag them over the new "Enemy 1" parent entity in the Entity Outliner window.

Next, right-click in the viewport or the Entity Outliner window and select the "Create entity" option. This new entity will be the parent entity for the entities pertaining to the second enemy AI character. Right-click this new entity and select the option "Open Pinned Inspector." In the "Name" input field, input the value "Enemy 2."

In the Entity Outliner window, hold down the Ctrl button on your keyboard, and this time, select all entities that relate to your second enemy artificial intelligence, once again excluding the AiTrigger and the AiNavigationArea entities. For my game example, these entities would be "AiSpawner2" and "AiWaypoint" entities 5 and 6. When all of the second AI enemy associated entities are selected, drag them over the new "Enemy 2" parent entity in the Entity Outliner window.

While this is a fairly organized structure for our enemy entities, we could potentially still have a cluttered Entity Outliner window when the number of entities increases. Because of this, we need to create a parent entity that will contain all of our enemy AI characters.

Right-click in the viewport or the Entity Outliner window and select the "Create entity" option, then open the Pinned Inspector for this entity by right-clicking it and choosing the option "Open Pinned Inspector." Rename the entity to "Enemies," by entering the value "Enemies" in the "Name" input field in the Pinned Inspector.

In the Entity Outliner window, hold down your Ctrl button on your keyboard, then select all enemy AI entities that you have created, this time *including* the AiTrigger and AiNavigationArea entities. For my game example, these entities would be "Enemy 1," "Enemy 2," "AiTrigger," and "AiNavigationArea."

With your enemy entities selected, drag these entities into the "Enemies" entity. If you have followed the steps correctly, your Entity Outliner window should be extremely organized and will allow you to collapse all enemy AI-related entities into a single row on the Entity

Outliner window. For larger and more complex projects, grouping entities in this manner helps organize the overall game development. The structure will look similar to Figure 7-12.

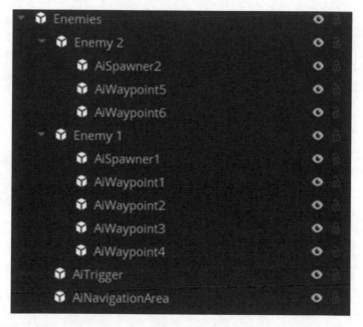

Figure 7-12. *The organizational structure of our enemy AI should have one parent entity that holds all enemies, and enemy parent entities that hold entities relating to specific enemies*

Congratulations, you have now added enemies to your game. Your player character will now have an objective – stay alive and silence the enemy. In the next chapter, we will look at the Lua scripting language and see how we can utilize it to edit some of our scripts to add new properties to components, change what certain input buttons will affect, and more.

CHAPTER 8

Beginning Lua Scripting

To add custom functionality for input controls, enemy controls, and other various gameplay values, we need to harness the powers of the Lua programming language. In this chapter, we will first have a programming in Lua crash course, then we will look at in-game examples for Amazon Lumberyard. In these examples, we will modify our player character's camera control script as well as the enemy AI spawner script.

In the crash course, we will learn about comments in Lua, both writing and invoking functions, loops, collections, variables, conditional statements, operators, and of course – classes. While this may not be enough information to write entire software packages or suites in the Lua language, it will give us a good enough basis to edit and manage game scripts. In the beginning of this chapter, we take a break from working directly in Amazon Lumberyard and explore the Lua programming language, ending the chapter with examples that directly affect our in-game components.

To follow along with the code examples in this chapter, begin by selecting "Tools" in the menu bar of Amazon Lumberyard, followed by selecting the "Lua Editor" option. With the Lua Editor tool open, select the "File" option in the menu bar, followed by the "New" option. A new file will be created that you can use to follow along in the book.

© Jaken Chandler Herman 2019
J. C. Herman, *Beginning Game Development with Amazon Lumberyard*,
https://doi.org/10.1007/978-1-4842-5073-0_8

The more we modify game scripts provided to us by Amazon Lumberyard, the more proficient we will be in both the Lua programming language as well as writing custom game scripts for Lumberyard. Do not be discouraged if this chapter of the book is harder for you to understand or follow at first. In time, your understanding for programming concepts will develop into a skill that you feel comfortable using. If you are already a programmer, this chapter should be a breeze for you – giving you a new language to harness at the same time.

Comments

The first aspect of Lua we will discuss is comments. Comments are annotations in source code that is easily readable by other programmers. Comments are typically added to take notes within the source code about the code to follow and are ignored by compilers and interpreters.

To create a comment in your Lua code, prefix your comment with two dashes ("--"), followed by a space, then your comment. For example, if I wanted to say "this is a comment" inside of my source code, I would type it as follows:

```
-- this is a comment:
```

The comment will be ignored by compilers and interpreters. Comments are a great way to write code descriptions as well as algorithmic descriptions inside the source code so other programmers do not need to reference external documentation. Because of this, we sometimes need to write comments that extend to multiple lines. To do this, after your two dashes, instead of placing a whitespace character, place two opening square brackets ("[") followed by your comment. To close the comment block, suffix your comment with two closing square brackets ("]"). For example, if I wanted to write a comment that says "Author: Jaken Herman

/ The following code controls character spawning", I would write the following:

```
--[[ Author: Jaken Herman
 The following code controls character spawning
 ]]
```

Variables

To store values within our code, we can define a *variable*, which associates an identifier, or name, with the value and assigns it to a storage location in memory. These variables can hold many different types of values, including functions, which we will discuss later.

Variable identifiers can be composed of alphanumeric characters as well as the underscore character, but no other special characters are syntactically correct. These identifiers must start with either a letter or an underscore character and never a digit.

Because Lua is a case-sensitive language, so you must be wary of upper and lowercased characters. In other words, a variable named "VariableA" cannot be referenced by calling "variableA", because the "V" in the beginning of the variable name is capitalized, while the "v" in the variable reference is lowercase.

While in many programming languages we must declare the type of data the variable will store, we do not need to do so in Lua, as the language is dynamically typed, so variables themselves do not have types – but the values they store do. Not only can values be stored in variables, but they can also be passed into functions as parameters, and they can also be returned as results from functional operations.

There are eight basic types of data that a Lua value can be, and you can wrap a value in the Lua function "type()" to discover the type of the given value. For example, you could run "type(true)" and receive the value "boolean" back.

Lua Data Types

Nil	Similar to "null" in other programming languages, nil is used to determine whether or not the value has data or no data.
Boolean	A Boolean type is a simple true or false state. These values are typically used for checking conditions, which we will discuss later in the chapter.
Number	The number data type represents floating point values.
String	Strings are used to represent an array of characters. Every word in this book would be considered a string.
Function	We will discuss functions later in the chapter. Functions represent methods written in Lua and help perform more complex tasks. This includes various computations and algorithms.
Userdata	The userdata data type offers an area in memory with no predefined operations in Lua.
Thread	thread data types are used to represent threads of execution that do not depend on one another and are used to implement routines that run in tandem.
Table	Represents arrays, sets, records, graphs, and other types of basic collections in Lua. Tables can hold any value except for a nil value.

Although Lua variables do not have data types, there are three types of variables depending on the scope of the variable:

- A global variable is a variable that is accessible by the program as a whole. All variables are considered to be global unless they are explicitly typed as local variables.

- A local variable is one that is declared with the keyword "local" and whose scope is limited within the functions inside their scope.

- The third type of variable is a table field, which, as stated earlier, is a type of variable that can store anything except for a `nil` state.

Variables are first defined, then initialized. This process can either be carried out on two different lines or on one line at the same time. For example, to define a local variable named "`my_variable`", we would write the code as follows:

```
-- variable definition:
local my_variable
```

The next step in the variable declaration process would be to initialize the variable. To initialize a variable that is already defined, we would write the code as follows:

```
-- variable initialization
my_variable = "this is my variable"
```

As stated earlier, we can merge this process into one line of code, definition, and initialization simultaneously. To do so, the code would look like this:

```
-- variable definition and initialization at the same time:
local my_variable = "this is my variable"
```

As stated before in this section, we can wrap a value in the Lua function "`type()`" to get the type of the value. For another example of that function invocation, let us see what a Lua interpreter will give us back when we invoke "`type()`" with the parameter "`my_variable`":

```
>> local my_variable = "this is my variable"
>> type(my_variable)
>> string
```

Because "my_variable" is an identifier that points to a location in memory storing the value "this is my variable", what really gets passed into the "type()" invocation would really be "type("this is my variable")". Because "this is my variable" is an array of characters, which is what a string data type is defined as, the type function returns back "string".

Conditionals

A conditional is a structure that a programmer can use to only perform an action in code if a particular condition, or set of conditions, is met. To perform these conditional checks, we can use if/else statements. To write an "if" statement, just type the word "if", followed by a conditional check encapsulated in parentheses, followed by the word "then". After the "then" comes the code you would like to run if the condition is met.

"if" statements can also be followed by "else" statements, which will execute some other block of code if the condition in the "if" statement is not evaluated to be true. The "else" statement is completely optional, however. Another optional addendum you can make to your "if" statement is an "elseif" statement, which will make another evaluation. You can combine as many "elseif" statements to your code as you would like.

Regardless of whether or not "else" or "elseif" statements are used, you always close out if/else statements with the "end" keyword. Let us look at an example of conditional statements in Lua. We will first declare a variable "my_variable" and assign it to the value 50. We will then check if the value is greater than 90 which, of course, it is not. We will make another check to see if the value is less than 45 which, again, it is not. Finally, we will resort to the default code being executed in the "else" statement, as no conditions were met:

```
local my_variable = 50

if( my_variable > 90 )
then
 -- execute this code if my_variable is greater than 90
elseif( my_variable < 45 )
then
 -- execute this code if my_variable is less than 45
else
 -- if neither previous condition is true, execute this code
end
```

It should be noted that if/else statements can be "nested" inside of another if/else statement. For example, if you make one conditional check, in the code block that should then be executed, you could make another check within that code block.

Operators

Based on the previous section regarding conditionals, Lua operators are essential in creating the checks needed in those code blocks. For example, in our if/else statements we used the less-than and greater-than symbols to check conditions. While these operators' uses are inherent, there may be certain operators that are not as simple to use. For example, what if in the preceding example, we wanted to check to see if my_variable was equal to 50?

We cannot do "if(my_variable = 50)", because a single equals sign denotes assignment (setting the value to 50 in this case), not equality comparison. To check equality, we would use the double equals sign (==). To correctly check if "my_variable" was 50, we would execute the following code:

```
if( my_variable == 50 )
```

Now, what if we wanted to check if "my_variable" was explicitly *not* 50? To check non-equality, we would use the symbol tilde followed by an equals sign. For example:

```
if( my_variable ~= 50 )
```

These are just two of the six relational operators in Lua. Relational operators will always evaluate to a boolean data type. In other words, every time a relational operator is used, the data that will be returned by the evaluation will be either true or false. The following table shows all of the relational operators with a description of what each of them do.

==	Checks if the value of the left-side quantity and the right-side quantity are equal.
~=	Checks if the value of the left-side quantity and the right-side quantity are not equal.
<	Checks if the value of the left-side quantity is less than the value of the right-side quantity.
>	Checks if the value of the left-side quantity is greater than the value of the right-side quantity.
<=	Checks if the value of the left-side quantity is less than **or** equal to the value of the right-side quantity.
>=	Checks if the value of the left-side quantity is greater than **or** equal to the value of the right-side quantity.

Relational operators are not the only types of operators in Lua, however. There are also logical operators and arithmetic operators. Logical operators are another group of operators whose values will always be evaluated to a boolean (true/false) data type.

Logical operators are typically used in connection with relational operators or with variables that hold Boolean values. A list of the three logical operators is as follows.

---

and   *If both of the operands represent something that is true, the condition becomes true. If only one condition is true and the other is not, the condition becomes false. In other words (true and true) = true, while (true and false) = false. This is clearer in the context of an* `if` *statement. If I only want a code block to execute if a number is less than 50 and greater than 25, this operator comes in handy:*
`if( my_variable < 50 and my_variable > 25) then ...`

or   *If at least one of the two operands represent something that is true, the condition becomes true.*

not   *This operator is used to reverse the logical state of its operand. In other words:*
`not false`
will evaluate to true.

Finally, the arithmetic operators supported by the Lua language are similar to typical everyday arithmetic operators.

+   *Computes the sum of the left-hand quantity and the right-hand quantity.*

-     *When used between two operands, this operator subtracts the right-hand quantity from the left-hand quantity.*
      When used to the left side of one operand, this "unary" operator will act as a negation, i.e., –50.

*   *Computes the product of the left-hand quantity and the right-hand quantity.*

/   *Computes the quotient of the left-hand quantity and the right-hand quantity.*

%   *Provides the remainder after a division has been performed on the left-hand quantity and the right-hand quantity.*

^   *Computes the exponent result of the left-hand quantity and the right-hand quantity.*

Loops

Suppose you have a block of code that you would like to execute multiple times until a point in which a condition is met. Statements inside the loop will be executed in sequential order. There are three main loop types that Lua provides programmers. The following table defines each of the loop types, and later in this section, we will provide examples of each.

while	*A while loop will repeat a code block, while the condition in question is true. When the condition in question becomes false, the code will terminate.*
for	*A for loop will repeat a code block X amount of times, where X represents a variable that will either increase or decrease as the code block executes. This will be further explained later in the section.*
repeat until	*The repeat until loop will execute a given block of code until a point in time in which the condition in question is met. This is similar to a while loop, although a while loop is guaranteed to execute at least once.*

Loops can be nested inside of another loop. In other words, you can use one or more loop inside of any other loop type. One thing that should be considered heavily when implementing loops is the concept of an *infinite loop*. An infinite loop is a loop that will not terminate, as it does not provide any exit routine. In other words, the condition in which the loop should stop can never be met. The loop will repeat continually until the operating system running the code terminates the program. If your loop should create a certain number of objects yet errors out and becomes an infinite loop, your computer may be bogged down by the new lack of memory (as more and more objects will be created as the loop continues).

While Loop

As stated earlier, the while loop allows you to repeat a block of code so long as the condition in question is true. For example, if I wanted to loop through every number from 1 to 10 and print the result out, I would write a while loop as follows:

```
i = 0
while(i <= 20)
do
 print(i)
 i = i+1
end
```

As you can likely tell, my "i=i+1" statement is what keeps the while loop from being an infinite loop. Without that statement, this block of code would continue to print "0". But because I incremented our variable, we can guarantee that the loop will not enter into an infinite state, and it will print each number from 1 to 20.

For Loop

For loops are interesting, as they allow you to declare and initialize control variables from within the for-loop syntax. In the "while" example earlier, we had to declare and initialize our "i" variable before using it in the loop. For loops have this step built in, and thus they are better suited for looping through values 0–20. For loops are the best control structure to repeat a block of code a specific number of times.

The syntax may be slightly confusing at first, but it gets easier the more you use it. Directly after writing "for", this is where you declare and initialize your control variable. To follow our preceding example, we would put "i=0". The next step is where you declare how many times your loop should run.

If your loop should count in descending order, this is where you would put your minimum value, whereas if your loop will count in ascending order, this is where you would put your maximum value. In other words, for our example, we want our "i" value to increase in ascending order, so we need to place the max value here, which is 20.

The last step of a for loop is to define how much your control variable needs to increment or decrement. For example, in our last example of our "while" loop, we had to add in a statement that said "i = i+1". Well, in our for loop, we simply need to put "1" in the top of our loop to declare that our control variable should increment by 1. If we were looping in descending order, we would put -1 in this value.

Let us take a look at the for-loop syntax, which will again count the numbers from 0 to 20:

```
for i = 0,20,1
do
 print(i)
end
```

The preceding code will do the exact same thing that our while loop did in the previous example, but this allows us to make the code block inside the loop a bit more succinct. What if we wanted to count in descending order from 20 to 0 while only printing even values? In this case, instead of decrementing by 1, we would want to decrement by 2 so that our code does not print any odd values.

The code for this is similar to our code in our ascending-order example, and in fact, we do not even need to modify the code block, we simply need to modify the first line of our for loop:

```
for i = 20,0,-2
do
 print(i)
end
```

Repeat Until Loop

Similar to a "while" loop, the repeat until loop is slightly different from both "for" and "while" loops, as the condition the compiler will check against is at the bottom of the loop instead of the top.

Syntactically, all you need to do for a repeat until loop is write the word "repeat", followed by the code block you would like to execute. Once you are done defining the code that will be repeated, place your "until" condition at the bottom of the code.

If the condition is false, the code will run again until the condition is evaluated to be true. Let us take a look at a repeat until code example solving the same problem as our other two loops have – printing all numbers from 0 to 20:

```
i = 0
repeat
 print(i)
 i = i + 1
until( i > 20 )
```

As you can tell, we once again had to declare and initialize the variable outside of our loop structure as well as increment and modify the variable from within the loop. The reason this loop can be dangerous at times is because developers may often overlook that they need to increment the control variable, at which time an infinite loop would be created.

Arrays

If you need to store a collection of data within a variable, you could use an array. An array is a collection of ordered objects. These arrays are implemented using tables that can be accessed by integer-based indices.

Array sizes are not fixed, so we can add as many values to these arrays as we would like, assuming that our system provides us enough memory to store the amount of values that we need to store.

To create an array that holds the string values "banana," "apple," and "orange" stored in a variable called "`fruits,`" we would write the code as follows:

```
fruits = {"banana", "apple", "orange"}
```

The preceding array is an example of a one-dimensional array. This is a simple table structure that could be viewed and interpreted as the following table.

1	banana
2	apple
3	orange

Notice that my index in the preceding table starts at "1." For most programming languages, arrays indices begin at 0, but in Lua, indexing will generally start at index 1. It is possible, however, to create objects at index 0, and, in fact, it is also possible to create objects that would be negatively indexed. For example, if I wanted to store a fruit value in our fruits array in the index location -1, I would write the code as follows:

```
fruits[-1] = "kiwi"
```

I would not suggest this; I would suggest that you stick to the standard default indexing that Lua provides, but I wanted to at least explain the options that are available to you. Assuming we did not modify our `fruits` array to add the kiwi, we could loop through our `fruits` array to print each fruit contained within by running the following code:

```lua
for i = 1,3,1
do
 print(fruits[i])
end
```

What if we only had two fruits in our array but left our for loop in the preceding example the same? While many other programming languages would throw an exception and terminate the code execution, Lua will return back a "nil" value if an array index is out of bounds.

Keep in mind that because arrays can store any data type, that means that arrays can also store instances of themselves. In this situation, you would be creating what is called a *multidimensional array*. To create a 2D array that contains fruits with their colors, you could write the code as follows:

```lua
fruits = {
 {"banana", "yellow" },
 {"apple", "red" },
 {"orange", "orange" }
}
```

In this case, if we knew "apple" was in position fruits[2], to get the color of that fruit, we would access it by the code:

```lua
fruits[2][2] -- evaluates "red"
```

So, if we wanted to loop through each of our fruit, print out the name of the fruit followed by the color of the fruit, we could nest a for loop and access our multidimensional array as follows:

```lua
for i = 1,3,1
do
 for j = 1,2,1
 do
```

```
print(fruits[i][j])
 end
end
```

The preceding code will yield the results:

```
banana
yellow
apple
red
orange
orange
```

Functions

A function in programming is a block of code that is grouped together to perform a specific task. If you have one large program that runs your code sequentially, you can likely break some of the tasks up into functions – especially the code blocks that are repetitive.

We have actually been using a function in all of the previous code examples, perhaps without you even knowing it. We have been invoking the "print()" function which, of course, takes in a parameter of any data type and outputs the string value of that parameter to the console.

All functions are invoked the same way, by typing the name of the function, followed by a set of parentheses. You may notice, however, that not all functions require data to be passed into them. Data passed into functions are known as "arguments" or "parameters." Functions are not required to accept parameters unless they are explicitly defined to accept them. To make a function called "add()" that takes two parameters (number_a and number_b) and returns the sum of these two values, we would write the code as follows:

```
function add(number_a,number_b)
 result = number_a + number_b
 return result
end
```

When using "add()", we would need to assign the result to a variable for it to be meaningful. For example, to get the result of 2 + 3 and store it into a variable called "my_sum", we would write the following code:

```
my_sum = add(2,3)
print(my_sum) -- will print "5"
```

We also need to keep in mind that variables declared and initialized within a function will not be accessible in other areas of our code, as the variable would be out of scope. The "result" variable in our example will only be accessible in our "add()" function, as it is scoped to exist within that block of code.

We can also pass in functions as parameters to other functions. Let us say we wanted to write a custom print function that would print out "The result of your function call is : ____", where the blank space would be filled with whatever the result of the function call is. First, let us define a custom function called "resultPrint()":

```
function resultPrint(result)
 print("The result of your function call is :", result)
end
```

Then, if we wanted to pair this with our call to "add()", we would modify add() to call our function instead of returning the result. Our end product would look like this:

```
function add(number_a,number_b,resultPrint)
 result = number_a + number_b
 resultPrint(result)
end
```

```
function resultPrint(result)
 print("The result of your function call is :", result)
end
```

Now, even though the "result" variable is scoped to our "add()" function, because we pass it into another function as a parameter, it is available for use in another function. This time, instead of saving the result of "add()" and calling "print(my_sum)" like our previous example, we can just execute the code like so:

```
add(2,3, resultPrint)
```

Classes

Classes allow you to make a model for creating objects that share common traits such as properties and methods. For example, if we use the example of "animal" for a class, we can provide properties for the sound the animal makes and the color the animal is.

Let us define an example Animal class code block that has a function called "getSound()":

```
Animal = {}
function Animal:new(o, sound, color, name)
 o = o or {}
 setmetatable(o, self)
 self.__index = self
 self.sound = sound
 self.name = name
 self.color =color
 return o
end
```

```
function Animal:getSound()
 print("The ", self.name, " goes ", self.sound)
end
```

Now that our class is defined, we can create a new Animal object. In order to define an object that will represent a black dog (which, of course, makes the noise "bark"), then get the sound that our dog makes in a formatted order, we would write the code as follows:

```
a = Animal:new(nil, "bark", "black", "dog")
a:getSound()
```

Because classes are so reusable and customizable, we begin to see their usefulness when it comes to game development. For example, in Chapter 7, when we selected a Lua script file to be linked with the Lua script component on our enemy AI spawner, more definable properties were added to the component. This happened because the code that we linked with the component declares those properties as necessary properties that the AI spawner would use. If we look at the following code, we see that these properties are defined in the aispawner class. Building onto that, we see what type these properties should hold, whether they be boolean, string, or number values. We also see that these values have default values set, so we do not place the burden on the game developer to necessarily have to define these.

```
local aispawner =
{
 Properties =
 {
 Enabled = { default = true },
 OverrideDebugManager = { default = false },
 GroupId = { default = "", description = ". . ." },
 AlertId = { default = "", description = ". . ." },
 SpawnInCombat = { default = false, description = ". . ." },
```

```
Teleport =
{
IsTeleportedIn = { default = false },
SpawnEffect = { default = "SpawnTeleportIn", description =
". . ." },
SpawnDelay = { default = 0.5, description = ". . .",
suffix = " s" },
SpawnDelayVariance = { default = 1.0, description = ". . .",
suffix = " s" },
DelayBeforeActualSpawn = { default = 0.5, description =
". . .", suffix = " s" },
},

DeathMessageTarget = {default = EntityId(), description =
". . ."},
DeathMessage = {default = "", description = ". . ." },
},

Data_GroupCountForAlive = "_alive";
Data_GroupCountForActive = "_active";
Data_GroupCountForDead = "_dead";
}
```

The preceding code, of course, is not the full `aispawner` class, but it is a portion of the class definition, and it is the only part that we will modify. In my game, when my enemy is to spawn, I would prefer that the enemy spawn immediately rather than have the half-second delay.

To enforce this, let us change the default value on the `"SpawnDelay"` variable within `aispawner.Properties.Teleport` to 0. To modify this value, either open the file within your favorite text editor, or use Amazon Lumberyard's built-in code editor. Right-click your enemy AISpawner entity, and choose the option "Open Pinned Inspector." In the component list, find your Lua script component, then next to your script input, select the button that is denoted by the icon that looks like a set of braces ("{}").

When you click this button, a new window will appear titled "Lua Editor," and changes to the script file may now be made. The "SpawnDelay" change we would like to make will be on line 17 of the provided AISpawner.Lua file. Use the keyboard key-combination Ctrl+S to save your changes.

Custom Inputs

As you create your own games, you will likely want to hook up custom input events to your character or your camera controller. For my example game, I would like to create an input event to reset the camera to its default location and height. Amazon Lumberyard's scripts for the camera controller allows you to zoom in and out of your character by pressing the keypad number 8 and the keypad number 2, respectively. We are going to create a custom input that allows you to press the keypad number 0 to reset the camera to its default settings.

To begin, within the Entity Outliner window, right-click your camera entity which will exist within the slice "PlayerSlice_EMFX," then select the option "Open Pinned Inspector." In the "Add Component" list, find the component named "Lua Script-CameraController," then open the script in the Lua Editor window by clicking the button whose icon is a set of braces.

Within the `cameracontroller:OnActivate()` function (Line 73), add the following two lines of code below the existing code:

```
self.debugNumPad0EventId = GameplayNotificationId(self.
entityId, "NumPad0", "float");
self.debugNumPad0Handler = GameplayNotificationBus.
Connect(self, self.debugNumPad0EventId);
```

Then, within the `cameracontroller:OnEventBegin()` function (Line 523), add the conditional check code inside of the existing conditional check for whether or not the TransitionTimer property is less than or equal to 0.0 (roughly line 571 of cameracontroller.Lua):

```
elseif (busId == self.debugNumPad0EventId) then
  self.CurrentSettings:CopySettings(self.TransitionToSettings);
  debugCamMovement = true;
```

Use the keyboard key-command Ctrl+S to save your changes to the camera controller script, then close the Lua Editor window, returning to the Amazon Lumberyard Editor.

Next, with the Pinned Inspector still open for your camera entity, click the "Add Component" button to add a new Lua script to the entity. Search for "Lua Script" in the search bar, then select "Lua Script" to add the component to your entity.

In your newly added Lua script component, click the button indicated by three dots next to the "Script" input to search for the script file you would like to link. In the "Pick Lua Script" window, search for "held.Lua", then click the orange "OK" button in the bottom right-hand corner of the window. Two new properties will become available to you at this point – IncomingInputEventName and OutgoingGameplayEventName. In both of these input fields, type "NumPad0". Close the Pinned Inspector for your camera entity.

The final step in adding custom camera inputs to your game is to modify the input manager that the camera controller references. In the Entity Outliner window, within your "PlayerSlice_EMFX" slice, right-click the entity named "InputManager," then select the option "Open Pinned Inspector."

In the list of components on your "InputManager" entity, find the "Input" component. To the right of the input labeled "Input to event bindings," select the button whose icon is a joystick, directly to the right of the "browse" button. This button will open the "Input Bindings Editor." In the input bindings editor, click the "+" button to the far right of the "Input Event Groups" item to add a new input event group.

By default, your new input event will be named "<Unspecified Event>." Scroll down to this event, then expand it by clicking the triangle to the left of the name of the input event. There will be two options for you to modify: Event Name and Event Generators. In the "Event Name" input, type "NumPad0".

To the far right of the "Event Generators" input, select the "+" button to add a new event generator. A new window will appear titled "Class to create." Make sure the drop-down for the class type has the value "Input" selected, then click the "OK" button in the bottom right-hand corner of the screen.

Now that an event generator exists, you will need to expand the "Event Generators" input in order to modify your newly created generator by clicking the triangle directly to the left of the event generators group. By default, the generator will be set to "gamepad_button_a," but as we would like this to be for the keyboard numpad 0 button, we need to modify this. Expand the "gamepad_button_a" generator, then change the "Input Device Type" to "keyboard." In the "Input Name" field, change the drop-down box to have the value "keyboard_key_numpad_0" selected.

Leave the "Dead zone" input at 0.2, as it will default to, but change the "Event value multiplier" input to 0.1 to match the other inputs for the keyboard numpad. Use the keyboard key-command Ctrl+S to save your input bindings changes. You have now successfully created the keyboard mapping to reset the camera. If the steps have been followed appropriately up to this point, your new input binding should look like Figure 8-1.

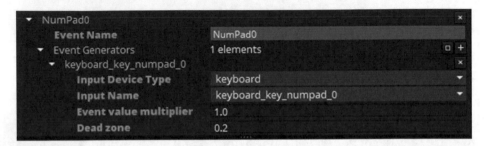

Figure 8-1. *The NumPad0 input binding **must** have the Input Device Type set to "keyboard" and the Input Name set to "keyboard_key_numpad_0"*

Now, click the "Play Game" button and experiment with your new custom input binding. To test your inputs, first use the keypad number 2 if you have one on your keyboard in order to zoom out from your character, then press the keypad number 0 to reset your camera to its default settings.

This chapter served as a crash course in the Lua programming language that was not necessarily intended to teach you how to create large software suites in Lua, but rather it was intended to teach you enough to be able to interpret and modify Lua scripts that Amazon Lumberyard provides, at which point you will learn to create your own scripts over time.

You should also take time to experiment with the input bindings to make your game support popular gaming controllers.

CHAPTER 9

Polishing Your Game

We have now finished going over how to modify scripts available within Amazon Lumberyard and how to create custom scripts. Now with our fully functional game, we can polish it and add details to make it stand out. For this chapter, we will solely be using assets that are provided by the Amazon Lumberyard engine including lens flares, game sounds, and particle managers that are built *specifically* for the enemy AI and player character slices we have been utilizing up to this point.

Lens Flare

The technique of using a lens flare has become fairly common within the past few years, mainly due to its ability to introduce a sense of realism into images, games, and video. An artificial lens flare mimics what happens when light (usually from the sun) is distributed in a camera's lens system.

To add a lens flare to our game to add a layer of authenticity, we first need to create an empty entity that will house our lens flare component. To do this, right-click in either the viewport or the Entity Outliner window and choose the option "Create entity."

Right-click your newly created entity and select the option "Open Pinned Inspector." In the Pinned Inspector window, in the input box to the right of the label "Name," type "Lens Flare" to name your entity.

© Jaken Chandler Herman 2019
J. C. Herman, *Beginning Game Development with Amazon Lumberyard*,
https://doi.org/10.1007/978-1-4842-5073-0_9

Once your entity is appropriately named, click the "Add Component" button to open the list of available components to add to an entity. In the "Rendering" component group, select the "Lens Flare" component, or alternatively type "Lens Flare" into the search bar in order to drill down to the component faster, then select the component to add it to your lens flare entity.

Now in the "Lens Flare" component you have just added to your entity, select the button indicated by three dots directly to the right of the input labeled "Library." A new window will pop up titled "Pick Lens Flare."

Find the XML file "`sunlensflare.xml`" in the following directory:

`MyFirstGame\libs\flares\`

Alternatively, you could find the file by typing "`sunlensflare.xml`" in the search bar directly under the "Pick Lens Flare" window title. Select the file, as shown in Figure 9-1, then click the orange "OK" button in the bottom right-hand corner of the screen.

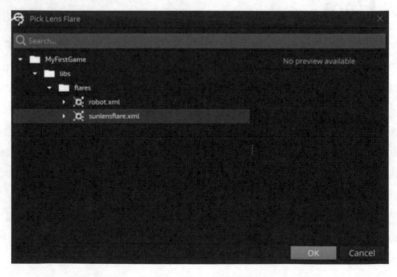

Figure 9-1. *Amazon Lumberyard provides two options for lens flare XML files. For our sunlight lens flare example, we want to use sunlensflare.xml, as shown here.*

Now, in the input box directly to the right of the input labeled "Library," you should see "sunlensflare." In the next input area, labeled "Lens Flare," the drop-down box will contain two different values for our use. By default, the "Lens Flare" input value will be set to "LensFlares.ChromaticRing," and for our example, this is the flare I will choose to use. Feel free to experiment with this input and change the option to "LensFlares.SunFlare" to see which you prefer.

Next, in the input group "Flare Settings," we should change the "Size" field to "2.5" rather than the default value "1" in order to make our lens flare more dramatic. To position our lens flare to be attached to the sun, make sure that the checkbox next to the input labeled "Attach to sun" is checked.

The final modification I would like to make on our lens flare component is to give it a blueish hue. In the "Color Settings" input group, next to the right of the input labeled "Tint," click the white square to open the color picker. In the input labeled "Red" within the color picker, set the value to 102. In the inputs labeled "Green" and "Blue" within the color picker, set the values to 161 and 255, respectively. Once done selecting your color, click the "X" button in the top right-hand corner of the "Select Color" window.

If you have set up your lens flare component correctly up to this point, your component should look like Figure 9-2.

Figure 9-2. *The lens flare component should have the ChromaticRing lens flare selected, the size value set to 2.5, the "Attach to sun" checkbox checked, and the color tint to RGB value 102, 161, 255*

When playing your game, you may not immediately notice how much value your lens flare component adds to the overall level of detail within the game. To see what your game looked like before adding your lens flare component, uncheck the "Visible" checkbox in your lens flare entity's lens flare component temporarily, then click the play game button to play your game. Point your camera up at the sun and move it around a bit, then press escape to exit your game. Re-enable the lens flare component by setting the "Visible" checkbox to be checked, then repeat the previous steps. You should notice a nice, professional looking lens flare within your game. Your before and after should look similar to Figure 9-3.

Figure 9-3. *The lens flare component will add an extra layer of detail and professionalism to your game. On the left was our game before adding the lens flare, and on the right is our game with the lens flare component added.*

Particle Manager

Next, we will add the particle manager slice that has been provided to us by Amazon Lumberyard. While this particle manager is tightly linked to the slices and entities that have been provided, you can always take this manager and link it to other entities such as other guns that you have created.

The particle manager is a slice that provides a wide array of visual effects in your game like while you are shooting or hit effects like where the bullet impacts. This will improve the experience of the combat system within the game as well as the overall feel of the game.

To add the particle manager slice, open your Asset Browser window by navigating to the top menu bar and selecting "Tools," followed by "Asset Browser." In the Asset Browser window, navigate to `MyFirstGame\slices\particle_manager.slice`, or search for `"particle_manager.slice"` in the

search bar at the top of the Asset Browser window. Once you have selected
"particle_manager.slice", drag it into either the viewport or the Entity
Outliner window.

No positioning is required for the particle manager to work as
intended, so at this point, we are done. Use the keyboard key-command
Ctrl+S to save your level, then click the "Play Game" button to see your
particle manager in action.

If the particle manager was added correctly, you will notice a charred
effect on walls (among other various hit effects), as well as bullet-emission
effects as shown in Figure 9-4. On the left side of Figure 9-4 is what
happened before adding the particle manager, and on the right side is what
happens when the particle manager is present in your game.

Figure 9-4.   *The particle_manager.slice slice provides a high level of
detail and polish to our game by adding visual effects when certain
actions occur*

While this pre-packaged particle manager slice is tailored specifically for the guns, AI characters, and player character also pre-packaged by Amazon Lumberyard, we can easily reuse this slice in our own games with custom guns, characters, and AI characters.

Upon further inspection of this particle manager, we see that it is merely made up of particle spawners. In other words, it is made up of entities that have a spawner component associated that will spawn some other slice which has the particle component associated with it. These particles are made up of XML files exactly like the birds.xml particle file we used in Chapter 6.

If you select the ParticleManager drop-down, you will notice that the particle manager contains a slice called "ParticleSpawner_LaserEnd." If we open the Pinned Inspector for this slice, it contains a spawner which spawns the slice "ParticleLaserEnd." When we open the inspector for the slice "ParticleLaserEnd," we will find a particle component that uses the particle effect library "weaponfx" with an emitter set to "Explosions. LaserImpact". There are also scripts involved with each of these slices which are modifiable for the user.

If we select the drop-down for this particle effect library, we can see the wide array of options we have at our disposal, such as lazer muzzles, lazer enemy impact, and more. To edit and extend these particle effect libraries, we need to first open the particle editor.

To open the particle editor, in the top menu bar of Amazon Lumberyard, select "Tools," followed by "Particle Editor." In the particle editor, we need to specify which particle library we would like to make changes to. For our example, we are going to change the WeaponFX library and change the coloration and size of some of the particle emitters.

When our laser makes impact with an object, instead of being a small white explosion, let us make it be a larger pink explosion, to add some more color and size variation to our game. Keep in mind, you can change as much about these particle libraries as you would like, but for my example, I will only be changing the colors. Before we move on, I would also like to point out that this editor is also where you will add more emitters to extend certain particle libraries. These changes will then be reflected in the XML file that the particle components reference. We will get to that later in the chapter.

To import a particle library to the particle editor, click the "File" option in the top menu bar of the particle editor window, followed by "Import." Alternatively, you can also use the keyboard key-command Ctrl+I. A new window will appear titled "Pick Particles." In this window, navigate to MyFirstGame\libs\particles, or search for "weaponfx.xml", and select "weaponfx.xml". When you have the WeaponFX particle library selected, click the orange "OK" button in the bottom right-hand corner of the screen.

Now, in the "Libraries" pane of your particle editor, you will see the different WeaponFX emitters that have already been created. Because we want to change the color of the laser on impact of an object, select the "LaserImpact" emitter that exists in the "Explosions" emitter group.

In the "Attributes" pane, this is where we can make changes to rotation, size, coloration, and other customizable options. Click "Particles" inside the attributes pane of the particle editor window to open the particle options group.

Next to "Color," select the color picker and change the color to whatever color you would like – in my example, I will be using a pink color. Close the color picker, then click "Size" inside the attributes pane of the particle editor window to open the size options group.

Next to the "SizeX" label, change this input to "5." Notice how the "SizeY" and "SizeZ" values also get updated. This is because the "Lock Aspect Ratio" checkbox is selected. If you would like your laser impact emitter not to be the same size on all axes, deselect the "Lock Aspect Ratio" checkbox.

Once you have made these changes to the LaserImpact particle emitter, your attributes pane for "LaserImpact" in the particle editor window should look like Figure 9-5.

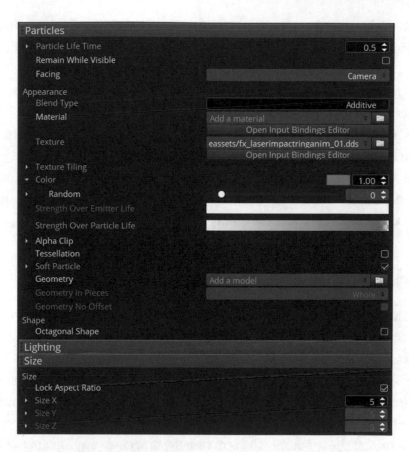

Figure 9-5. *Particle emitters are extremely customizable. The image shows that we have changed the color and size of the LaserImpact emitter. Note that the "Texture" and "Material" for this particle emitter can also be changed here.*

Use the keyboard key-command Ctrl+S to save the changes. When you close the particle editor and run your game, you will now see that when shooting a wall or some other object, the impact of your laser will now be a larger pink explosion rather than a small white explosion.

These changes, however, will not look the same when shooting an enemy AI. To make these changes match on impact of an enemy character, you need to make the same changes you made to the LaserImpact particle emitter on the LaserImpactEnemy particle emitter.

To add a new emitter to the Weapon FX particle library, reopen the particle editor by going to "Tools" in the menu bar, followed by "Particle Editor." Reimport the Weapon FX library if needed, then under the "WeaponFX" library in the "Libraries" pane, right-click an empty area and hover over "Add new," then select the option "Add particle."

A new particle emitter will then be created, and you can customize which materials and textures you would like in the "Particles" option group in the "Attributes" panel. This emitter, upon saving the Weapon FX library, will be available in the emitters drop-down menu in particle components when the Weapon FX particle library is selected.

Audio and Sound Effects

The player character slice as well as the enemy slices and various other environment slices we added to our game already have certain sound effects associated with them. Because Amazon Lumberyard is still in development, however, sometimes the project configurator does not move over all necessary assets when the "StarterGame" gem is added to your project – and thus, you may not hear these associated sound effects.

To import these sound effects manually, first close any instances of the Amazon Lumberyard Editor that you have open, if any. Next, open a Windows Explorer window, and navigate to the StarterGame directory located here:

```
Amazon\Lumberyard\<Lumberyard-Version>\dev\StarterGame
```

Click the folder named "Sounds," then right-click and select the "Copy" option, or use the keyboard key-command Ctrl+C to copy the folder that contains all of the provided sound effect assets.

Next, navigate to your MyFirstGame project directory, located here:

```
Amazon\Lumberyard\1.17.0.0\dev\MyFirstGame
```

Right-click inside your directory, and select the "Paste" option, or use the keyboard key-command Ctrl+V to paste the folder containing the provided sound effect assets into your MyFirstGame project directory.

Once the assets have been manually imported to your MyFirstGame project, reopen the Amazon Lumberyard Editor, and click "Play Game." Your game will now have all sound effects that are associated with the slices it contains.

To create sounds of your own, or to modify the sound effects that Amazon Lumberyard has provided, you will need to utilize the Audiokinetic Wwise LTX software that Amazon Lumberyard includes in the Lumberyard Setup Assistant. As this tool is out of the scope of this book, we will not discuss specifics on how to use it; rather, you should use the provided Wwise LTX documentation by opening the "Wwise LTX Authoring Tool," then pressing "F1."

To polish our game audio a bit further, let us discuss the Audio Area Environment component. Suppose in our game we have a cavern. In this cavern, all triggered sounds should have a reverberating effect, as the sound waves would bounce off of the cavern walls. To do this, we first need to establish a trigger area.

To begin, either in the viewport or the Entity Outliner window, right-click and choose the option "Create entity." Right-click your newly created entity, and select the option "Open Pinned Inspector." Inside the Pinned Inspector window, change the "Name" input to "ReverbTrigger," so we know what this entity will represent.

Next, click the "Add Component" button, and under the "Scripting" component group, select "Trigger Area," or search for "Trigger Area" in the search bar at the top. Once the trigger area component has been added to your "ReverbTrigger" entity, we need to also supply the required shape component that will be the outline of the trigger area. Press the "Add Required Component" button inside the trigger area component, then choose "Box Shape."

By default, your Box Shape component will be small – 1x1x1 meters. Because this area is meant to represent a cave or cavern, this area will need to be large – as large as the cave itself. If you do not have a cave created in your game yet, that is ok – you can make on later. For now, we will have to use our imagination and say that the cave is 20 meters on all axes. In the Box Shape component, change the "Dimensions" for X, Y, and Z all to "20.0m".

Once your box shape and trigger area have been created, move your ReverbTrigger entity to an area on the map in which you would like to have a reverberating sound effect on all audio events that are triggered.

The second step to the process of adding audio area environments is creating another entity that links to the trigger entity we just created. To do this, right-click in either the Entity Outliner window or the viewport, and choose the option "Create entity." On your newly created entity, right-click and select "Open Pinned Inspector."

In the "Name" input field, change the default entity name to "ReverbEffect." Next, click the "Add Component" button, and under the "Audio" component group, choose "Audio Area Environment," or just search for "Audio Area Environment" in the search bar at the top of the window.

Similar to the trigger area component we just added, the Audio Area Environment component will also require a shape component to be added to the entity as well. Click the "Add Required Component" in the "Audio Area Environment" component pane, and choose the option "Box Shape." By default, the dimensions of this box shape will also be 1x1x1 meters, but to match our trigger area's Box Shape component, we will change the dimensions for the x-, y-, and z-axes to "20.0m".

In the "Audio Area Environment" component, find the label "Broad-phase trigger area," then next to that input, choose the button whose icon is a reticle in order to use the picker tool. With the picker tool enabled, click the "ReverbTrigger" entity you created earlier in this section. This will link the Audio Area Environment component to the ReverbTrigger area.

Finally, next to the input labeled "Environment Name," choose the browse button, whose icon is three dots. A new window will appear labeled "Choose Environment...." Navigate to startergame/_envFX/reverb, or search for "reverb" in the search bar at the top of the window. Select "reverb," then click the gray "OK" button in the bottom right-hand corner of the window.

If all steps have been followed correctly up to this point, your Audio Area Environment component as well as your Box Shape component on your "ReverbEffect" entity should look like Figure 9-6.

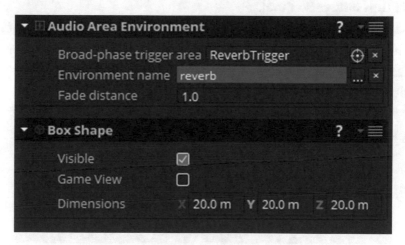

Figure 9-6. *A reverb effect will now be heard when our player character enters the area defined by the ReverbTrigger entity*

Click the "Play Game" button, or use the keyboard key-command Ctrl+G to play your game now. Enter the ReverbTrigger area, and listen to the reverberating sound effect on all triggered audio within this area.

Because these two entities are linked together, for organizational purposes it is best if we reduce them to one item in the Entity Outliner window. To do this, right-click inside the Entity Outliner window or the viewport, and choose the option "Create entity." Right-click this newly created entity, and choose the option "Open Pinned Inspector."

Change the "Name" input for this entity from the default name to "Reverb." Close the Pinned Inspector. Next, drag both the ReverbTrigger entity as well as the ReverbEffect entity into the Reverb entity to make the Reverb entity a parent of the two.

Alternatively, to make the parent-child link between these entities from within the Pinned Inspector window, right-click either the ReverbTrigger entity or the ReverbEffect entity, and choose the option "Open Pinned Inspector." In the transform component of this entity, to the right of the "Parent entity" input, choose the button whose icon is a reticle in order to enable the entity picker tool.

With the entity picker tool enabled, click the "Reverb" entity we just created. This will create parent-child link between the selected entity and the "Reverb" entity. Repeat this step for whichever entity you did not initially select between the two reverb-related entities.

If the preceding steps were followed appropriately, your "Reverb" entity should look similar to Figure 9-7 in the Entity Outliner window.

Figure 9-7. *Keep related entities grouped by creating a parent-child link between them*

We have now added a bit of polish to our game. It is looking professional – but there is one final step we need before we can call this game complete: a user interface.

CHAPTER 10

Setting Up a User Interface

When we run our game, the level starts immediately. However, you can imagine most modern games typically start with a title menu with the name of the game as well as a button we can click to start the gameplay. In this chapter, we will explore the process of creating a user interface (UI) using canvases, Script Canvases, and the UI Editor. Before we begin, we first need to make sure that UI assets provided by Amazon Lumberyard are in our game project. While we will be creating our own user interface rather than using the provided UI, we still need to bring these assets over, as the player character contains a head-up display that would be beneficial to gameplay.

To obtain these assets, first navigate to your MyFirstGame project directory, located at

```
Amazon\Lumberyard\<Lumberyard_Version>\dev\MyFirstGame
```

If you have a folder in this project directory named "UI" that both exists and is not empty, feel free to skip to the next section in this chapter. If you either do not have this folder in your project directory, or the folder is empty, follow these next few steps.

Navigate to the Amazon Lumberyard StarterGame directory, located at

```
Amazon\Lumberyard\<Lumberyard_Version>\dev\StarterGame
```

© Jaken Chandler Herman 2019
J. C. Herman, *Beginning Game Development with Amazon Lumberyard*,
https://doi.org/10.1007/978-1-4842-5073-0_10

Select the "UI" folder, then right-click it, and choose the "Copy" option. Alternatively, you can select the "UI" folder and use the keyboard key-command Ctrl+C to copy the UI folder to your clipboard.

Once the folder has been copied, navigate back to your MyFirstGame project directory, right-click inside the directory, and choose the "Paste" option – or just use the keyboard key-command Ctrl+V to paste the UI folder into your project directory.

Now any UI elements that are referenced by the player character slice will be present when running "MyFirstGame."

Creating a Canvas

To begin working on our start screen, we first need a UI canvas to work with. To begin, we first need to open the UI Editor. There are a few different ways to open the UI Editor. The first is to navigate to the "Tools" menu in the top menu bar of Amazon Lumberyard's editor and choose the option "UI Editor." The second option is via the Editors toolbar by clicking the UI Editor button ( ). To open the Editors toolbar, right-click any area inside the toolbar area and make sure the "Editors toolbar" option has a check mark next to it.

Once the UI Editor has been opened, we need to create a new canvas file. To do this, click "File" in the menu bar at the top of the UI Editor window, followed by the "New Canvas" option, or just use the keyboard key-command Ctrl+N.

In the "Hierarchy" pane of the UI Editor window, we need to add a slice from the slice library provided by Amazon Lumberyard. The slice we need to add is a text element that will display the name of our game to the user.

Right-click inside the hierarchy pane and choose the option "New," followed by "Element from Slice Library," once again followed by "Text." You will notice that more options have now become available to you in the "Properties" pane of the UI Editor; this includes "Text," "Color," "Font size," and more underneath the "Text" properties category on the right side of the editor window.

Now you can style your game title and name your game. For this example, we are going to use a red text that says "My First Game" in large 64-point font. In the input box next to the "Text" label, I will change the default "My string" to "My First Game." In the color picker directly to the right of the "Color" label, I will change the RGB input value to "255, 0, 0". Finally, in the "Font size" input to the right of the "Font size" label, I will change the default "32.0" to "64.0".

Because we will be adding another element to this canvas, we are going to move the title text from the center. To change this, in the "Top" input of the "Anchors" section, I will change the default value from "50%" to "25%." Feel free to move the title to wherever you think may fit your game style. If your text element was added correctly to your canvas, it should look similar to Figure 10-1.

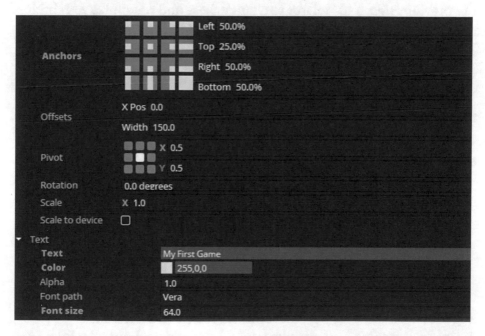

Figure 10-1. *The text element on your UI canvas is one of the first things your player will see upon entering your game. Make sure it looks nice!*

The next thing we need to add to our canvas is a button element that, when clicked, will begin our game. To do this, right-click in the hierarchy pane and select the "New" option, followed by "Element from Slice Library," followed once more by "Button."

In the hierarchy pane, you will notice that the button element contains a text element nested within it. This text element holds the button label, which defaults to "Button." To change this to "Start Game," click the text element that is a child of the newly added button element. In the properties pane, in the "Text" properties group, change the input labeled "Text" from the default "Button" to "Start Game." Keep in mind here you could also make adjustments to the text coloration, size, font, and all other text-based attributes you could change in the previous text element.

Back in the hierarchy pane, select the button element we just added in the previous step, and feel free to change these and customize your button to your liking. Once you have customized the button to your liking, we will add a little bit of functionality to it. We need to add a click action that will start the game when the button is clicked. In the button properties "Button" group, under the "Actions" array, in the input labeled "Click," add the text "StartGamePressed".

If the steps were followed correctly, your button actions properties should look like Figure 10-2.

Figure 10-2. *Adding the "StartGamePressed" click action is important for this button to be useful – we will find out why later in the chapter*

Save your canvas by using the keyboard key-command Ctrl+S or by navigating to "File" in the menu bar, followed by "Save Canvas As." Name your canvas "StartScreenCanvas" in the MyFirstGame\UI directory, and make sure that the "Save as type" is "*.uicanvas". Close the UI Editor window.

Creating a Script Canvas

Script Canvas is a chart-based scripting environment that is used to create game behaviors and logic within Amazon Lumberyard. The main advantage to the Script Canvas environment is that you can use it to create scripts for your game's logic without knowing how to code.

To begin, open the Script Canvas editor by selecting "Tools" in the top menu bar of Amazon Lumberyard, followed by "Script Canvas." As this Script Canvas environment is a visual-based way to create scripts, I will first explain the necessary steps, then follow each step with a figure so you are able to visualize what the Script Canvas chart should look like.

To start a Script Canvas, we first need to add an "On Graph Start" node which does not require an input to function. To do this, in the node palette, navigate to the "Utilities" node group and find "On Graph Start," or type "On Graph Start" in the search bar within the node palette. Drag the "On Graph Start" node into the empty area that currently says, "Use the File Menu or drag out a node from the Node Palette to create a new script." The area will now be replaced with a Script Canvas with one node element – the "On Graph Start" node – as shown in Figure 10-3.

Figure 10-3. *The "On Graph Start" node will be the start to our UI Script Canvas*

An important thing to consider is that Script Canvases need to be thought of as "flows." For example, what happens after our "On Graph Start" node is the next "step" in sequence and it needs to be linked to the "Out" parameter on the "On Graph Start" node. To link two nodes, connect the "Out" parameter of the previous node to the "In" parameter of the next node.

In our example, the next node we need is the "Load Canvas" node so we can load the canvas we just created after our game begins. In the node palette, find the "Load Canvas" node by navigating to the "UI Canvas Manager" node group or by typing "Load Canvas" into the search bar within the node palette. There are two different "Load Canvas" node options. The "Load Canvas" node we need is *specifically* filed under the UI Canvas Manager node group. Select this node and drag it into our Script Canvas, and connect the "Out" parameter of the "On Graph Start" node to the "In" parameter of the "Load Canvas" node by clicking and dragging between the two.

In the "Pathname" input on the load canvas node, input the file path to the canvas we just created in "MyFirstGame\UI". Because the game assets are stored in the "MyFirstGame" directory, it is only necessary to begin the path with "UI," so for the example canvas we created earlier, this "Pathname" input would be "UI\StartScreenCanvas.uicanvas".

If all steps have been followed correctly up to this point, your Script Canvas will now look like Figure 10-4. Note the link between the "Out" parameter of the "On Graph Start" node and the "In" Parameter of the UI

Canvas Manager "Load Canvas" node. If this link does not exist, the Script Canvas flow will not work correctly and the execution of the flow will be abruptly stopped.

Figure 10-4. Linking the "On Graph Start" node with our "Load Canvas" node will load the canvas provided in the "Pathname" input after the game has started

If you were to add this Script Canvas to an entity at this point, the created canvas would appear, but any input events from the user would not be captured appropriately. We do not want our user to be able to play the game while the start menu is still visible. For this reason, we need our canvas to consume all input events (keyboard button presses or mouse clicks).

To enable this functionality, in the node palette, find the "Set Is Consuming All Input Events" node by navigating to the "UI Animation" node group, or by typing "Set Is Consuming All Input Events" into the search bar within the node palette. Drag the "Set Is Consuming All Input Events" node into the Script Canvas, and attach the "Out" parameter of the "Load Canvas" node to the "In" parameter of the "Set Is Consuming All Input Events" node.

This node specifically requires two links to be made. Because the "Set Is Consuming All Input Events" node requires a source to know when to consume input events, we need to link the "Canvas EntityID" variable on our canvas loader node to the "Source" variable in our input consumer node. Finally, we need to ensure that the checkbox next to the "Consume" label is selected.

If all steps have been followed correctly up to this point, your Script Canvas should look similar to Figure 10-5. Note here, not only is the "Set Is Consuming All Input Events" node linked to the "Load Canvas" node by input and output parameters, it is also linked by the "Canvas EntityID" variable on the canvas loader and the "Source" variable on the "Set Is Consuming All Input Events" node. Also note that because the "Load Canvas" node is already linked to the "On Graph Start" node, we do not need to link the "Set Is Consuming All Input Events" node to the "On Graph Start" node directly.

Figure 10-5. *Because our "Load Canvas" node is already linked to the "On Graph Start" node, we do not need to explicitly link our new "Set Is Consuming All Input Events" node to it. Our input consumer node is linked to the canvas loader node by both input/output parameters and by the entity id and source variables. Make sure the "Consume" checkbox is checked!*

Now that input events will be consumed and our cursor can be used to select our "Start Game" button, we need to ensure that the cursor is visible to the user. In the Script Canvas, the value determining whether or not our cursor is visible is by a counter that presumably defaults to 0. If the cursor's visible counter is 0 or below, the cursor will not display. If the cursor's visible counter is greater than 0, the cursor will be displayed. In our logic flow, we need to increment the cursor visible counter by 1 after the "Set Is Consuming All Input Events" node is fired.

In the node palette, navigate to the UI cursor node group and find "Increment Visible Counter," or just search for "Increment Visible Counter" from within the search bar in the node palette. Drag the "Increment Visible Counter" node into our Script Canvas, and link the out parameter of "Set Is Consuming All Input Events" to the input parameter of the "Increment Visible Counter" node. If these steps were followed correctly, your Script Canvas will now look like Figure 10-6.

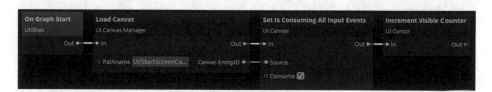

Figure 10-6. *The "Increment Visible Counter" node is required to have a visible cursor in your user interface*

Now that our cursor is visible – we need to finally link our "Start Game" button to our Script Canvas. To do this, we need to add an "On Action" node that will listen for action events on a given canvas.

In the node palette, navigate to "On Action" in the "UI Canvas" node group, or just search "On Action" in the node palette search bar. Drag the "On Action" node into the Script Canvas. In the node inspector pane for this node, ensure that the "Display Connection Controls" checkbox is selected as shown in Figure 10-7.

Figure 10-7. *The "Display Connection Controls" property on the "UI Canvas / On Action" node must be selected to hook up action events*

Next, connect the out parameter of the "Load Canvas" node to the "Connect" parameter of the "UI Canvas" node that is a parent of the "On Action" node. Also connect the "Canvas EntityID" variable on the "Load Canvas" node to the "Source" variable on the "UI Canvas" parent node.

If all steps have been followed up to this point, your Script Canvas should look like Figure 10-8.

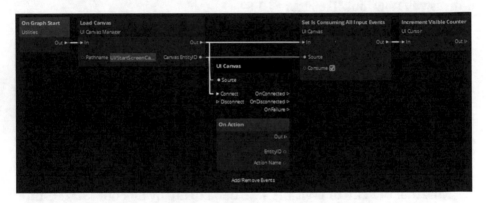

Figure 10-8. *No changes were made to the "On Action" node in this iteration of the Script Canvas, but rather in the "UI Canvas" node that is a parent node of the "On Action" node*

Because we only have one canvas button and thus only one action to listen for, we can move forward in our Script Canvas without having to specify which action we are listening for. When the "Start Game" button is clicked, we want to hide the start screen and allow the user to begin playing our game.

To do this, we need to add an "Unload Canvas" node to our Script Canvas. In the node palette, in the "UI Canvas Manager" node group, look for "Unload Canvas," or just search for "Unload Canvas" in the search bar of the node palette. Drag the "Unload Canvas" node into the Script Canvas we have created up to this point.

Hook up the "OnDisconnected" parameter of the "UI Canvas" node to the "In" parameter of the "Unload Canvas" node. Also link the "Out" parameter of the "On Action" node that exists within the "UI Canvas" node to the "In" parameter of the "Unload Canvas" node. Lastly, link the "Canvas EntityID" from the "Load Canvas" node to the "Canvas EntityID" on the "Unload Canvas Node."

If the steps were followed correctly up to this point, your Script Canvas should look similar to Figure 10-9. Keep in mind, as we add more and more nodes, this Script Canvas will get slightly more complex, and the links may be harder to follow from here on out.

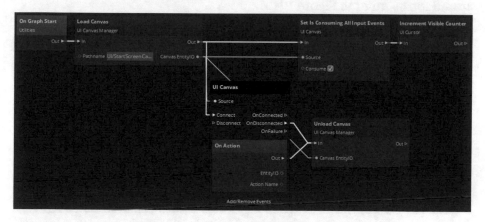

Figure 10-9. *The Unload Canvas node will have two input connections, from the UI Canvas OnDisconnect property as well as the ouput property on the On Action node. The Canvas EntityID needs to be linked with the Load Canvas node so that the same canvas that was loaded is unloaded.*

Now when our "Start Game" button is clicked, our canvas will unload, and we can begin to play our game. There is one problem, however. Our UI cursor will still be visible while playing our game, because our UI cursor's visible counter will still be set to a value greater than 0.

The "Set Is Consuming All Input Events" property will automatically be unloaded because it was tied to the "Load Canvas" node, which was linked to the "Unload Canvas" node. To decrement our UI cursor's visible counter when the UI canvas is unloaded, we need to add one final node – "Decrement Visible Counter."

To begin, in the node palette, under the "UI Cursor" node group, look for the node named "Decrement Visible Counter," or just search for "Decrement Visible Counter" from the search bar within the node palette. Drag the "Decrement Visible Counter" node into the Script Canvas, and link the "Out" parameter from "Unload Canvas" to the "In" parameter of the "Decrement Visible Counter" node.

If the steps were followed correctly up to this point, your Script Canvas should look similar to Figure 10-10.

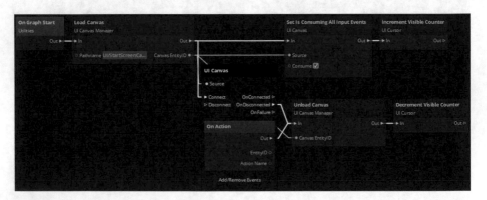

Figure 10-10. *The "Decrement Visible Counter" node needs to have its input parameter linked with the "Unload Canvas" node's output parameter. In this case, when the UI canvas (our start screen) is unloaded, our UI cursor will no longer be visible, as our player will be ready to play the game.*

To save your Script Canvas, click the "File" menu option in the menu bar within the Script Canvas editor, then select the option "Save As." Name your Script Canvas "StartScreenScriptCanvas" inside the MyFirstGame\ scriptcanvas directory, and make sure the "Save as type" is set to "*.scriptcanvas" and close the editor.

Adding the Script Canvas to Our Game

To add the Script Canvas we just created to our game, we first need an entity to house the Script Canvas component. Right-click in either the Entity Outliner window or the viewport, and select the option "Create Entity."

Right-click this newly created entity, and choose the option "Open Pinned Inspector." In the "Name" input, change the default name to "Start Screen" so we know what this entity represents later in development.

Click the "Add Component" button from within the Pinned Inspector for this "Start Screen" entity. Under the "Scripting" component group, click "Script Canvas," or just search for "Script Canvas" in the search bar of the "Add Component" window.

Next to the input labeled "Script Canvas Asset," click the browse button, whose icon is three dots in order to navigate to our newly created Script Canvas file. A new window will appear titled "Pick Script Canvas."

Navigate to MyFirstGame\scriptcanvas\StartScreenScriptCanvas. scriptcanvas, or just search for "StartScreenScriptCanvas". Select the "StartScreenScriptCanvas" option and click the orange "OK" button in the bottom right-hand corner of the screen.

Use the keyboard key-command Ctrl+S to save your level, followed by Ctrl+G to start playing your game. Notice how all inputs for your player character are ignored because your start screen is visible. This is due to the handiwork of the "Set Is Consuming All Input Events" node.

Click the "Start Game" button we created to dismiss the start screen, and begin playing your game. Your final start screen should look similar to Figure 10-11 if you followed all of the preceding steps exactly. Keep in mind that if you made customizations outside of what we changed within this text, your start screen may slightly vary in look and feel.

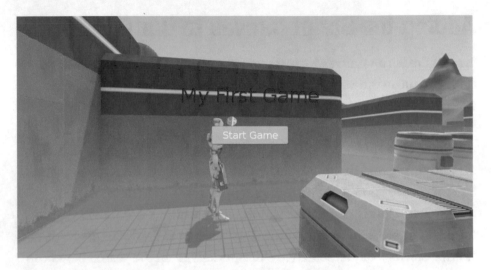

Figure 10-11. *Our start screen user interface displays the name of the game in large red text and provides a button to start the game. All input prior to clicking the "Start Game" button is consumed by the start screen.*

In this chapter we learned how to use the UI Editor as well as the Script Canvas editor to create UI canvases and Script Canvases. We learned how Script Canvases can be utilized to create game logic without the use of code and leveraged this functionality to create a start screen that will occur before gameplay does.

At this point, our game is as good as complete. We have a player character, enemies, props, sound effects, particles, vegetation, terrain, and even an interactive user interface. We are now on the final step – exporting the game so you can share it with your friends.

CHAPTER 11

Exporting the Game

You have done it. You have created your game. Congratulations! Now, all that is left for you to do is export that game so you can share it with your friends and family, or so you can upload it to an online portfolio that you can share with potential employers. In this chapter, we will walk through the steps necessary to export your game for PC, Xbox, and PlayStation platforms.

Creating a PC Build

Exporting your game to an executable file will package all necessary data files so that your game will be able to run without the need to have Amazon Lumberyard installed. To begin this process, first open Amazon Lumberyard.

With Amazon Lumberyard open, navigate to the top menu bar of the editor window, and choose the option "Game," followed by "Export to Engine." After the Amazon Lumberyard Editor exports the game to the engine, a pop-up alert will appear with the text "The level was successfully exported", as shown in Figure 11-1.

© Jaken Chandler Herman 2019
J. C. Herman, *Beginning Game Development with Amazon Lumberyard*,
https://doi.org/10.1007/978-1-4842-5073-0_11

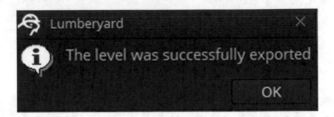

Figure 11-1. *If Amazon Lumberyard successfully exports the game to engine, this alert window will appear*

Click the gray "OK" button in the bottom right-hand corner of this alert window to dismiss it. At this point, it may seem as if nothing interesting happened, because your editor window will look the same as it did prior to exporting the game.

To see what happened when clicking "Export to Engine," we need to open the Windows Explorer file manager to find the game launcher executable file our editor just generated. This launcher file will be stored in the same directory as the "Editor.exe" executable file that opens our Lumberyard Editor.

If you are running Visual Studio 2015 or earlier, navigate to this directory, located at

`C:\Amazon\Lumberyard\<Lumberyard_Version>\dev\Bin64vc140`

If you are running Visual Studio 2017 or later, navigate to this directory, located at

`C:\Amazon\Lumberyard\<Lumberyard_Version>\dev\Bin64vc141`

Once in this directory, you may have to scroll for a while before finding the file named "MyFirstGameLauncher", as shown in Figure 11-2. If you named your game something other than "MyFirstGame", this file will be named whatever you named your game with the prefix "Launcher".

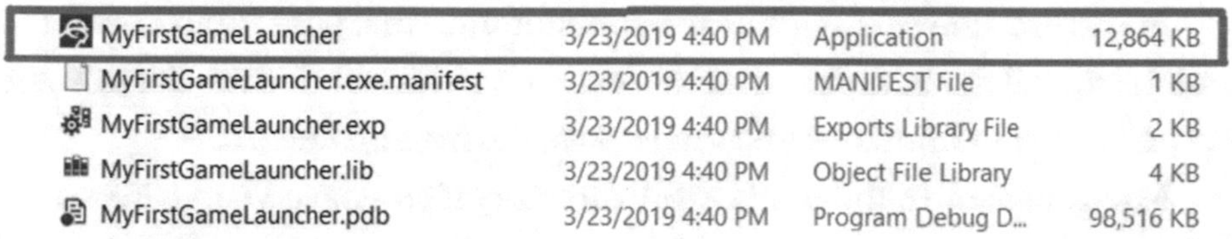

MyFirstGameLauncher	3/23/2019 4:40 PM	Application	12,864 KB
MyFirstGameLauncher.exe.manifest	3/23/2019 4:40 PM	MANIFEST File	1 KB
MyFirstGameLauncher.exp	3/23/2019 4:40 PM	Exports Library File	2 KB
MyFirstGameLauncher.lib	3/23/2019 4:40 PM	Object File Library	4 KB
MyFirstGameLauncher.pdb	3/23/2019 4:40 PM	Program Debug D...	98,516 KB

Figure 11-2. *The Executable File will have the extension ".exe" and a file type named "Application"*

Double-click this file to open your game. When you first run your game, you will notice that you are greeted with a black screen, no UI, no sounds, and no real indication of how to start your game. Here, we can open the developer console within our game to specify which level we would like to play. Keep in mind, we will learn how to set the default level later in this chapter, but it is necessary that you know how to manually change the level from within the developer console.

With your game launched, while looking at the black screen, press the tilde key (~) to launch the developer console. Type "map Level_1", or whatever you named your level, and wait for your launcher to load the level that you specified. Note here that the "map" command can be used to change levels at any point in your game.

This is not a great solution, however. When our player starts their game, they will be expecting a start menu and a default level to begin – not some blank screen and a console. To set the default level, or map, in the Lumberyard engine, we need to navigate back to our project directory, located at

```
C:\Amazon\Lumberyard\<Lumberyard_Version>\dev\MyFirstGame
```

In this directory, look for a configuration file named "autoexec.cfg". If this file does not exist, create it by using the "New item" button in the Windows Explorer window. If the file does exist, open the file in your text editor of choice.

In the first line of this autoexec configuration file, type "map Level_1", which will tell the launcher that the level named Level_1 is the default level to run when our launcher first loads. Save the file and close it.

Navigate back to the Bin64vc140 directory if you have Visual Studio 2015 or below or to the Bin64vc141 directory if you have Visual Studio 2017 or later, then double-click your "MyFirstGameLauncher.exe" file to relaunch your game. Now, your default level will be loaded, as shown in Figure 11-3, and your player can begin playing the game.

Figure 11-3. *Your completed game can now be opened as a stand-alone file*

Note   To exit your game, press the tilde (~) button to enter the developer console and type the command "quit."

Keep in mind that any further changes you decide to make in your game within the Amazon Lumberyard Editor will require you to repeat the preceding steps for exporting your game. If these steps are not repeated, any changes made to your game will not be reflected when launching the game from the launcher executable file.

Creating a Console Build

PC is a great gaming platform, but what about the consoles that are built solely to play video games on? Well, because Amazon Lumberyard is such a new platform, the process for building to Xbox and PlayStation requires certain steps that will be provided by Amazon.

Xbox

To begin debugging and building to the Xbox platform, you must first become a licensed Microsoft Xbox Developer. To become a licensed Xbox developer, you must first apply to the ID@Xbox program by visiting `www.xbox.com/en-US/developers/id/apply` and filling out the form. Information you will need to provide will be information about your studio such as company name, studio web site, engines used (Amazon Lumberyard), and more.

Once your application has been submitted, you will need to wait for Microsoft to respond to the application regarding your acceptance to the program. Upon your acceptance to the program, you will then need to e-mail your name, studio name, and the licensed e-mail address to lumberyard-consoles@amazon.com.

Amazon will likely respond within 2 weeks regarding your next steps in your Xbox development process. Because the process will differ from developer to developer, this is as much information as I can give on the subject matter. If Amazon has not responded to your request within 2 weeks, it is likely that your e-mail may have been buried in a backlog – so feel free to send a follow-up e-mail regarding the status of your inquiry.

A simple template for this e-mail for your use would look something like Figure 11-4.

To whom it may concern,

Per the Frequently Asked Questions page – (https://aws.amazon.com/lumberyard/faq/), I have provided my studio information below for review. Please advise me on the next steps I will need to take in order to begin building Amazon Lumberyard games to my Xbox locally for testing as well as the steps I will need to create a build for releasing my game.

I am a registered Microsoft Xbox Developer with the ID@Xbox program, and my studio information is as follows:

Name: (Your Name)

Studio Name: (Studio Name)

Licensed Email: (Email)

If there is any further information you need from me, please let me know at your earliest convenience.

I eagerly await your response,

(Your Name)

Figure 11-4. *A template for your e-mail to lumberyard-consoles@ amazon.com regarding Xbox development.*

PlayStation

To begin debugging and building to the PlayStation platform, you must first become a licensed Sony Interactive Entertainment Developer through the SIE DevNet Network. To become a licensed Sony Interactive Entertainment developer, you must first apply to the program by visiting `https:// partners.playstation.com/apex/PO_AccountAppliPTR?lang=en` and filling out the form. Information you will need to provide will be information about your studio such as company name, studio web site, proposed distribution types (physical, digital), and more.

Once your application has been submitted, you will need to wait for Sony Interactive Entertainment to respond to the application regarding your acceptance to the program. Upon your acceptance to the program, you will then need to e-mail your name, studio name, and the licensed e-mail address to lumberyard-consoles@amazon.com.

Amazon will likely respond within 2 weeks regarding your next steps in your PlayStation development process. Because the process will differ from developer to developer, this is as much information as I can give on the subject matter. If Amazon has not responded to your request within 2 weeks, it is likely that your e-mail may have been buried in a backlog – so feel free to send a follow-up e-mail regarding the status of your inquiry.

A simple template for this e-mail for your use would look something like Figure 11-5.

To whom it may concern,

Per the Frequently Asked Questions page – (https://aws.amazon.com/lumberyard/faq/), I have provided my studio information below for review. Please advise me on the next steps I will need to take in order to begin building Amazon Lumberyard games to my PlayStation locally for testing as well as the steps I will need to create a build for releasing my game.

I am a registered Sony Interactive Entertainment Developer through the DIE DevNet program, and my studio information is as follows:

Name: (Your Name)

Studio Name: (Studio Name)

Licensed Email: (Email)

If there is any further information you need from me, please let me know at your earliest convenience.

I eagerly await your response,

(Your Name)

Figure 11-5. *A template for your e-mail to lumberyard-consoles@ amazon.com regarding PlayStation development*

Final Thoughts

Completing a video game is not an easy task, so at this point, you should have a sense of pride that you were able to make it through the process. At this point, you can add more levels to your game in order to lengthen your user's gameplay time and make the game harder as the game progresses, keeping your player excited and challenged by your game.

You can also add more detail to your user interface or terrain. Perhaps this is the time when you explore multiplayer functionality or even cinematics. There is so much constant potential for improvement in your game development career. The one thing that is important throughout the entire process is that you should never stop learning.

Congratulations, you have just completed your very first game – as well as this book. Your journey is not over, however. This book will have given you the steps to get a brief introduction to game development in Amazon Lumberyard, and I hope you continue with your journey and create the next hit game.

Index

A

Amazon Lumberyard engine, 1
    custom installation, 6
        Get Started tap, 8, 9
        Lumberyard editor, 12
        optional SDK, 11, 12
        plugins installation, 11
        SDK download
          progress bar, 10, 11
        setup assistant, 6
        software fields, 8, 9
    express installation, 5
    installation, 4, 5
    required components, 1
    Visual Studio, 2–4
Animation Editor, 34
AnimGraph and actor
        components, 124–128
Arithmetic operators, 175
Arrays, 179–182
Artificial intelligence (AI)
    enemy AI navigation area,
        creation, 150–155
    enemy AI spawn point,
        creation, 155–158
    enemy AI trigger,
        creation, 146–150
Asset Browser window, 23

    EditMode toolbar, 25–28
    editors toolbar
        abstraction layer, 35
        buttons, 30
        far-left pane, 32
        material editor, 31
    file location, 23
    filter assets, 24
    material editor window, 33–37
    object toolbar, 28–30
    product files, 24
    selection, 23
    toolbar, 25
Attachment component, 128
    audio components, 129, 130
    camera components, 131
    editor, 132
    entities and slices, 129
    environment components, 132
    in-game cameras, 132
    PlasmaRifle slice, 128
Audio and sound effects, 200–204
Audio components, 129, 130
Audio Transaction Layer (ATL), 35

B

Beta, 14
Bitmap, *see* Raster image

© Jaken Chandler Herman 2019
J. C. Herman, *Beginning Game Development with Amazon Lumberyard*,
https://doi.org/10.1007/978-1-4842-5073-0